21st Century Communications

An Executive Guide to
Communications in the Enterprise

Andy Mattes and
Bob Emmerson

CAPSTONE

Copyright © 2003

The right of Andy Mattes and Bob Emerson to be identified as the author of this book has been asserted in accordance with the Copyright, Designs and Patents Act 1988

First published 2003 by
Capstone Publishing Limited (a Wiley & Sons Company)
The Atrium
Southern Gate
Chichester
West Sussex
PO19 8SQ
www.wileyeurope.com

Reprinted July 2003

All Rights Reserved. No part of this publication may be reproduced, stored in a retrieval system or transmitted in any form or by any means, electronic, mechanical, photocopying, recording, scanning or otherwise, except under the terms of the Copyright, Designs and Patents Act 1988 or under the terms of a licence issued by the Copyright Licensing Agency Ltd, 90 Tottenham Court Road, London W1T 4LP, UK, without the permission in writing of the Publisher. Requests to the Publisher should be addressed to the Permissions Department, John Wiley & Sons Ltd, The Atrium, Southern Gate, Chichester, West Sussex PO19 8SQ, England, or emailed to permreq@wiley.co.uk, or faxed to (+44) 1243 770571.

CIP catalogue records for this book are available from the British Library and the US Library of Congress

ISBN 1-84112-475-3

Graphics and production by Melis Graphic Services by www.melisgs.com
Printed and bound in Great Britain by TJ International Ltd, Padstow, Cornwall
This book is printed on acid-free paper responsibly manufactured from sustainable forestry in which at least two trees are planted for each one used for paper production.

> Substantial discounts on bulk quantities of Capstone Books are available to corporations, professional associations and other organizations. For details Telephone John Wiley & Sons on (+44-1243-770441), fax (+44-1243-770571) or email corporate development@wiley.co.uk

21st Century Communications

Adding value to your IP infrastructure
An executive guide to communications in the enterprise

The Authors

Andy Mattes is a Member of the Group Board of Siemens AG's Information Communication Networks (ICN) Group. In this capacity he is responsible for ICN's Enterprise Networks Business Unit's sales, marketing and manufacturing activities as well as regional responsibilities for Germany and Latin America. He was named to this position in January 2001. Andy joined Siemens in 1985 and has held various sales and management positions throughout Siemens AG. He can be reached at: andy.mattes@siemens.com

Bob Emmerson is an English national living in the Netherlands. He holds a degree in electronic engineering and mathematics from London University and now works as a freelance writer, part-time consultant and 'industry observer.' Bob writes about Information and Communications Technology for various technical and business publications. In addition he has produced three market reports for the Financial Times as well as a number of white papers. He can be reached at: b.emmerson@electric-words.org

Acknowledgements

The authors will like to acknowledge the assistance and advice in creating this publication given by Gadi Tamari and Peter Benedict, both from Radvision, as well as Mark Clark, Roman Ehrl, Michael Meyer and Tim Miller. Mark, Roman, Michael and Tim work for the ICN division of Siemens AG.

• Reviews

Reviews

"By focusing on real-life applications that are currently available (or available in the near future), the authors provide a realistic view of IP communications, looking at how and why enterprises will move to these new solutions. The book shows the value of IP communications and how companies can justify the migration - not based on the technology - but on how the technology can make companies more productive."

Blair Pleasant, President and Principal Analyst, COMMfusion, Santa Rosa, CA 95409

"The book presents a clearly-worded and cogently argued case for not only why but also how communications will revolutionize business in the future. It demonstrates that an increasingly complex world requires an increasingly sophisticated technological response to lower the cost of doing business. Readable and intelligent."

Matthew May, Editor, Communications International

"The promise of Internet Protocol telephony is as much misunderstood as it is misrepresented. It is, therefore, a refreshing change to find a book that takes a critical look at IP telephony and delivers the facts rather than sounding like an echo of the vendor-inspired marketing material that has in the past confounded the widespread comprehension of this emerging communications protocol.

In the book 21st Century Communications Andy Mattes and Bob Emmerson peel back the layers of confusion that have been wrapped around the issue of IP telephony over the past several years and lays out a concise view of the applications and solutions that can be enabled by IP communications. The authors further highlights the impact of IP-enabled communications on personal as well as corporate productivity while managing to avoid the sensationalistic hype that has typified any discussion of IP telephony in the past."

Paul Stockford, President and Chief Analyst, Saddletree Research, Arizona

Foreword

Technology never stands still; in fact, the pace of change always seems to be increasing. This makes it particularly hard for managers to focus on how technology can be best implemented in order to enhance their business processes, and in the past too many so-called solutions failed to deliver productivity and other business benefits. Today, however, a number of key technologies are literally converging and delivering real competitive advantage for business users. New applications will not just speed up critical business processes, but also allow management to look again at the fundamentals of their business and its core competences.

The catalyst for this has been the almost ubiquitous deployment of a common communications protocol for all media types: voice, data and video. Since the capability of transmitting voice in IP packets was first demonstrated in the mid nineties, tremendous commercial forces have been applied to development and refinement of this transport mechanism. We are now in a position to state —unequivocally — that IP communications is a reliable and resilient proposition for organizations and businesses of all shapes and sizes.

Cost, as ever, is an important consideration and returns on investments can be realized in acceptable timeframes — often it is under year. Just the ability to have one network for all communications tasks instead of two or more produces immediate opex savings. However, the business case rests on IP-enhanced applications and the stress-free increase in productivity that they deliver.

Ian Hunter, Editor, Comms Business Magazine

Contents

Preface I

Executive Summary 11

Chapter 1: Issues and explanations 29

> The difference between regular telephony and that of IP telephony and the issues that arise when planning and making the transition are covered. The intrinsic flexibility of the new medium is explained as well as the new communications concepts that are enabled.

Chapter 2: It's all about applications 45

> IP is enabling a totally new breed of synergistic, productivity-enhancing applications to be employed on phones, PCs and PDAs. This chapter also covers the shortcomings of today's point solutions and shows how communications portals are enabling smarter ways of working.

Chapter 3: Migration: the #1 issue 67

> Migration is the only significant issue: how to realize the productivity and other benefits of IP Communications and at the same time protect the legacy investment in regular telephony systems, phones and cabling.

Chapter 4: Phones, PDAs, and their amazing new functionality 83

> What is the look and feel of the new telephony interface; how do PCs enable easy use of advanced functionality and how do phones and PCs function as a single entity? In addition, this chapter examines the role of wireless communications in the office environment and 'hot spots'.

Chapter 5: Video enters the picture   93

    This time the V in VoIP stands for Video. This is a relatively easy media type to add to a converged network, the key parameter being bandwidth, which is not an issue. Video is being used to enhance desktop meetings and facilitate the use of this medium for international conferences, thereby minimizing the need to travel and attend 'in person'.

Conclusions   103

Appendix A: VoIP Services   107

Appendix B: ROIs   109

Appendix C: Standards and ubiquity   111

Glossary of terms   119

Preface

ROI: *Return On Investment*

The authors recognize the fact that the information and communications industry has been long on promises and short on delivery in recent years. Executives and managers have not seen the return on investments they expected, so they are naturally skeptical about new IT developments promising amazing ROIs. Yet at the same time the need to reduce overhead, boost productivity and improve competitiveness remains. In fact, in the current economic climate it is more important than ever. As we shall see in the executive summary, transaction costs represent well over 50% of GDP and the equivalent figure for the average enterprise is similar.

CRM: *Customer Relationship Management. Systems used to plan, schedule and control pre- and post-sales activities.*

This is a difficult business circle to square. There is a clear need to leverage those investments, e.g. communications enable mainstream applications such as CRM and a growing recognition that the corporate network is a source of competitive advantage. But — and it is a very big but — budgets are limited. Incremental investments that make big differences are clearly a more attractive option than forklift upgrades, as are ways of reducing operating expenses. Yet at the same time management needs to look further ahead; short-term tactics need to be combined with a longer-term strategy in order to stay ahead of the game.

ERP: *Enterprise Resource Planning. Originally a manufacturing system but one that now comprises virtually all related activities.*

A few years ago the fear of being left behind resulted in hasty purchases of expensive systems such as CRM and ERP. Today management are taking their time and examining the business case for new developments in much greater detail. The cases may stand up individually but they must also contribute to the business strategy, so this is not an easy task and mistakes will be costly. Moreover this is not something that can be delegated.

Detailed examinations cannot be undertaken without an uncluttered view of the underlying technology and the assumptions on which

• Preface

vendors base their business cases. Acronyms form part of that clutter and the need to promote individual agendas may be buried beneath some of the assumptions. Thus, there is a very real need to have a business-centric understanding of the technology developments that will enable and support your organization's activities in the near- and medium-term. This book will give you that understanding.

IP: Internet Protocol. The lingua franca of data communications.

A series of proven IP Communications developments are delivering those business objectives, i.e. reduced overhead, greater productivity and improved competitiveness. The first stage involves IP telephony and IP-enhanced real time applications, and at a later stage video enters the picture. It starts with video-enhanced desktop meetings, is normally followed by low-cost videoconferencing and then by mobile video telephony. We shall be outlining entry-level options that allow the benefits to be trialed and evaluated, as well as cost-effective migration routes.

The book covers the transition of voice from its traditional domain to that of a converged 'IP everywhere' environment. It will also make the business case in more detail. This transition has started in many enterprises around the world and those early adopters are already realizing the benefits.

We shall also take a look at long-term strategies. When voice and data have converged and significant benefits been realized what comes next? On the application front video multicasting is a logical development and further down the road there are other developments such as third-generation platforms that handle both mainstream business processes and real-time communications. The introduction of these platforms into all-IP environments will elevate the functionality and take the merger of information and communications to a higher level.

Much more than mere convergence

IP takes this rich, real-time medium back to its communications future. The human voice is the best way to convey subtle messages, to express feelings and emotions; it is also the optimal way to reach consensus. In recent years email has become the primary medium for business communications, but now these two very-different media types can start to complement each other in a number of exciting and innovative ways, e.g. listening to emails while mobile and dictating replies to the urgent messages. This simple example shows that voice and data are doing a lot more than merely converging, allowing one network to be employed for all media types. Voice is not simply morphing into another data type, it is set to become the most important communications medium on local and wide area networks. And that is one of the many ways that this development is able to leverage the considerable investments that organizations have made in their information and communications infrastructures.

> **PDA:** *Personal Digital Assistant, e.g. the Palm Pilot or HP-Compaq iPAQ.*

> *In IP environments voice is treated as another data type and telephony becomes an application running over the data network.*

IP is the language that virtually all computers speak, so convergence allows PCs and PDAs to have similar functionality to that of IP phones and the reverse is also true: IP phones become thin-client data devices. 'Thin' in this context means that they have less computing resources (memory, screen-size, etc). This indicates the need for a broader term than IP Telephony and IP Communications is the one that will be employed in this book.

> **USB:** *Universal Serial Bus. A PC interface used for low-speed peripherals.*

Turning a PC into a real-time communications device is done via software, hence the term 'softphone'. Modern desktop and notebook PCs have a multimedia capability so you can talk and listen to these machines. Alternatively a basic handset can be connected to the USB port. These are low-cost devices having a microphone and loudspeaker; calls are made and received via a graphical display on the PC. Softphones also enable easy access to corporate directories and the creation of personal directories; these are stored on the PC. Calls are made and forwarded simply by clicking on the relevant entry.

In addition, softphones can be used to complement the functionality of desktop IP phones. This allows easy use of advanced telephony features such as conference calls. For example, simply dragging the names of the relevant parties onto a conference call icon can set up a conference call.

The business case

Strategies and visions are based on medium- and long-term goals, but IP convergence starts with the delivery of immediate, tangible benefits that minimize operating costs and generate fast ROIs. True vision will therefore combine an informed view of the future with a practical approach based on current needs and budgets. In essence, it will ensure that corporate short-, medium- and long-term benefits are defined and realized. So, what are those benefits? Are they compelling? Make your own judgment.

The business case is founded on: (1) the ease with which communications applications are employed; (2) the stress-free increase in personal productivity; (3) faster, better ways of communicating and a reduced need to commute to the office; (4) the ability to respond quickly to changes in the market; (5) the intrinsic flexibility of IP based networks; (6) the ability to centralize and control all communications costs (including mobile calls).

The following pages will show how those six key benefits can be achieved by your organization. However, despite the fact that these benefits are tangible, changing the communication foundation of a company is something that has to be planned very carefully. Benefits have to be weighed against a certain amount of disruption, although this can be minimal when a good migration strategy has been formulated and implemented. This important subject will be covered in some detail.

One network

DOS: *Disk Operating System.*

Data processing and data communications are relatively new developments. In the 1960s we had mainframe computers and a proprietary, vertical environment, that of IBM. Mini computers came next; the architecture was peer-to-peer (horizontal) but this environment was also proprietary. Data was exchanged between peers over local area networks and then in the early 1980s the PC entered the picture. Open systems using de facto standards such as DOS, followed by Microsoft Windows and the client-server architecture took over and came to dominate the desktop. Thus, today's data world is very different to that of the 1960s. Systems have to be open and standards are everything.

PBX: *Private Branch Exchange. An in-house telephony system that connects, disconnects, and transfers calls.*

PBXs are termed first-generation platforms in this book.

The public telephone network has been in existence for a century or more and the ability to phone around the world is something we take for granted. In this domain standards are mandatory, otherwise the world's biggest machine would not function, but private switching platforms — PBXs — have not followed the open systems route. There are a number of valid reasons why this did not happen, the most important probably being the fact that they did an excellent job and there was no market call for anything to be changed. The architecture of phones and these proprietary platforms is vertical and it is very similar to that of mainframes; in fact, some analysts refer to PBXs as telephony mainframes.

We therefore have a vertical wireline telephony model and a semi-vertical wireless telephony model. It is semi-vertical because mobile phones can call wireline phones and vice versa. The data model, however, is horizontal; an email can be sent from a Windows PC to an Apple or a PDA. The sender does not know anything about the recipient's device. What real time IP Communications does is turn the regular telephony on its side and enable the PC model to be replicated. Replication also covers third-party development of applications and hardware becoming a commodity. In addition, and this is a very exciting concept, software modules (application components) can be shared by the worlds of voice and data, thereby eliminating the need to reinvent communications wheels over and over again.

A communications infrastructure that employs IP for all media types is also intrinsically flexible. PCs, for example, can be added and they self-configure; people move around the enterprise and have access to all authorized resources from any location. This enables 'hot desking' which reduces the amount of office space needed to operate the business. This level of flexibility is not practical with the vertical model of PBXs; it is possible, but it's an expensive, slow process. PBXs were not designed to perform these tasks, which are a relatively new requirement of today's business models.

New IP platforms run the new applications and productivity-enhancing applications are the driving force behind this development. This second step also facilitates interoperation between real time telephony and data-centric business processes. An upcoming third step will elevate the functionality of the network and allow real time communications to become a component of the Web services landscape. We are therefore migrating to one converged network that handles the traffic of all media types and then, at a later stage, making a second transition to next-generation platforms that handle both mainstream business processes and real-time communications.

We have proven technologies and robust systems that enable voice to be transported over IP networks without any appreciable difference in quality to that of the public network. The Internet Protocol enables this development, although the Internet itself is not used. Instead,

• Preface

VoIP indicates that the voice signal has been digitized and converted into the packet format used by IP.

IP PBXs provide similar functionality to legacy PBXs but employ a different switching technology. They are termed second-generation platforms in this book.

Voice over IP (VoIP) traffic is transported over well-provisioned, managed IP networks (LANs and WANs) and calls are processed by IP communications platforms (aka IP PBXs). Telephony traffic is given priority over data on these converged networks.

Point solutions

Today's enterprise communications landscape is complex. In many companies IT managers were not able to control the purchase of mobile devices such as PDAs; they were bought by individuals and put onto claims for expenses. (There is an analogy here to the early days of PCs). As a result these devices have made an unstructured, unmanaged entry into the enterprise and providing support has become very expensive. Individuals having technical skills are able to synchronize their PDAs with their PCs and even perform this task while mobile; others are less fortunate. They look to the IT department for help, but resources are stretched and this task has a low priority.

This is one example of a point solution that needs fixing. Cellular/mobile phones are another. Everybody gets a second phone number and a second voicemail box in addition to their email inbox. There are redundant messaging systems, multiple calling numbers and logon IDs, and virtually no intelligent control over the way we wish to be contacted. Telephone tag, for example, is something we have all experienced. In theory we are reachable anywhere, anytime, but in practice we tend to end up with voicemail. When the called party calls back they have the same experience and so it goes on.

IP communications platforms can be seen as another application server that resides on the same network.

Ironically, both parties may have been free at the time but have switched over to voicemail since anywhere, anytime is an intrusive concept. This is clearly a waste of time and money; however, it becomes a serious issue when one considers the difficulties of setting up meetings and conference calls.

SMS: Short Message Service.

Instant messages are a relatively new development, particularly for the corporate environment.

We have the technology: virtual personal assistants that try and find you; email, SMS, and IM (instant messages). We also have the devices: wireline and wireless phones, PCs and PDAs. And that is the problem. They are not joined up and there is no way of managing one's availability intelligently.

At first sight it may not be clear how IP Communications can change this scenario and as a media type it cannot. The breakthrough comes from the move towards open telephony systems; the ease with which communicating applications can be created and deployed; the use of application program interfaces (APIs) and standards, which open up the environment to third-party developers; and telephony's ability to replicate the client-server model of computing. For example, the goal of having just one virtual number has been realized. The system will try the desktop phone first and then the mobile, a simple process but one that makes a big saving on the phone bill. More calls get through the first time because the system knows your location on the network (telephony now functions the same way as email). More important calls get through because you can manage your availability, e.g. I'm in a meeting so only transfer calls from my boss and partner. Calls that don't get through go to the same voicemail system. All message types are unified and appear in the same inbox.

Too good to be true?

Maybe that's the way it sounds, but think back to the early days of the PC. We now have the equivalent of a mainframe computer on the desktop and similar processing power in a portable machine. Applications abound and we use them via intuitive graphical interfaces. PCs have become multimedia machines. We take these amazing developments for granted and why not. Being taken for granted is a sign of success.

The public telephony infrastructure has evolved into an ultra-reliable system.

In comparison, data networking is a relatively recent development and many wide area networks rely on parts of that infrastructure.

Twenty years later we are in a similar position with respect to real time communications. Telephony is transitioning towards an environment based on open standards having published APIs that enable third party development. Exactly how and when your organization will take IP Communications on board will depend on many factors, the most important being the need to protect legacy investments in PBXs, phones and cabling. But it is only a question of time, direction, and individual requirements.

The PC model will be followed as well as the more recent Web model and the implications for the industry are seismic. Hardware will become a commodity; functionality, applications and support services will become the core competences of the communications industry.

Man is a social animal

Let us step back from technology for a moment and take stock. Apart from the business benefits outlined earlier, what is the overriding rationale for IP Communications and what do we understand by that last word?

Communication is defined by Webster's dictionary as a process by which information is exchanged between individuals through a common system of symbols, signs, or behavior. Not just words. Indeed most cultures around the world teach their children the importance of looking at a person with whom they are communicating. In contrast, the most common form of punishment in the world is isolation. This is because communication is more than just transmitting words through voicemail, a telephone handset or an email. It is about expression, body language, attitude, appearances, impressions, instincts, gesture, motion and emotion. And it fulfils a basic human need; the majority of us need to interact with one another face-to-face, person-to-person. Were that not the case we should not be taking so many business trips and sitting in planes and airport lounges for so many hours.

However, in recent years email has become the primary medium for off-line business communications. Email is efficient and economic; it crosses time zones and transports attachments such as Word documents and PowerPoint presentations. We take this amazing media type for granted and it is a key enabler of the global economy, but email is a somewhat soulless way of communicating and its ease of use has led to abuse. Thus, although technology has improved the speed and efficiency of communications in many ways, it has also detracted from its basic qualities.

Gigabit Ethernet LANs run at 1000 Mbps (bits per second).

Earlier we referred to well-provisioned, managed IP networks and the need to prioritize voice traffic since this is a real-time medium, as is video. From a transmission perspective the only significant difference between voice and video is that of bandwidth. However, bandwidth has become a commodity and LANs can run at Gigabit speeds, so this is not a significant issue.

Video will therefore follow telephony and become an integral part of tomorrow's information and communications infrastructure. Thus, next generation communications will be interactive and multimedia. Video-enhanced applications will retain the global reach of the

Internet and email but incorporate personal values: the sight and sounds of personal interaction, the gestures and signals between people, the look on the other party's face.

Distance learning

Desktop multimedia conferencing will soon become both practical and cost-effective and the implications for the bottom line in terms of improved collaboration and reduced travel costs are obvious. Training and distance learning (aka e-learning) are applications that will follow on the heels of video to the desktop. Employees who travel to attend courses will principally be involved with trainers (people) as well as presentations and documents (files). These elements can be replicated, integrated and distributed when the underlying technologies and networks are the same. And once again, the savings in travel time and costs are considerable.

A shared vision

The two authors share this vision. Bob Emmerson has been writing about it for several years while Andy Mattes has been busy planning and managing the solutions that will deliver sound and sight at tomorrow's epicenter. This work has been conducted for Siemens, which is the world leader in traditional PBXs as well as the new converged platforms. However, this is not a PR publication. No reference is made to specific products and the guidance this book seeks to convey is objective, but we would like to point out that every benefit, claim and application is either a near- or medium-term deliverable.

Executive Summary

The book's sub-title — *"Adding value to your IP infrastructure. Developments no business manager can afford to ignore"* — is a bold statement but it is one that will be substantiated in non-technical detail, the focus being on the proven ability of IP-centric communications to lower costs, increase profitability, and deliver superior services to customers and prospects. Similar claims have been made in the past; many technology developments failed to deliver while others only addressed part of the problem. And all too often the cost and complexity of implementing so-called solutions exceeded the long-term benefit, i.e. there was no valid return on investment.

With the benefit of hindsight it is easy to see what went wrong. The industry became infatuated with technology and along the way it lost sight of the fact that technology was only a means to an end. Thus, the crisis of confidence that we are facing in 2003 is one that the industry created: the players are responsible for the result. For example, by the fourth quarter of 2002 the telecommunications value chain had turned into a loss chain; a handful of Internet carriers had incinerated almost 70 billion dollars worth of shareholder equity. In parallel we have witnessed a tide of confusion and frustration sweeping over the market; users are becoming technology-fatigued. Indeed, so-called solutions are often perceived as obstacles that get in the way of the real work.

In addition, assumptions about the Internet's ability to generate new revenue streams were erroneous and the dot.com economy collapsed with disastrous results. Traffic was generated but the Net did not pay its way; the industry did not manage to establish a sustainable IP value chain. However, there is light at the end of the tunnel and it is starting to shine with increasing luminance. IP and other Internet standards and technologies are enabling the deployment of next-generation networks that reduce communications costs significantly. Applications that are easy to use are being developed; in fact, usage is intuitive and one application builds on another to produce personal value chains. And mainstream business processes such as customer relationship management are being communications enabled and enhanced, which allows companies to deliver better services than their competitors.

"Adding value to your IP infrastructure" indicates that IP communications leverages a core asset: the organization's information and communications infrastructure. Value is added

• Executive Summary

via: (1) lower communications and network management costs; (2) IP-enhanced applications that enable better, smarter ways of working and communicating, thereby boosting productivity while reducing stress; (3) superior services such as contact centers and the virtualization of the call center concept; (4) the new ability to mix and match services that are managed internally with those of service providers.

Value-add number four, a relatively new development, can be used to extend the reach of the new applications to authorized third parties such as customers and suppliers as well as small branch offices and teleworkers. For example, customers using the same virtual private network will be able to check up on stock positions of products they require (a data app) while talking to their account manager (a telephony app) who could then go on to book an order and quote the delivery time. All this in real time.

In the past the ability of the former PTTs to offer anything other than baseline telephony was limited by the inherent limitations of the technology, but IP is intrinsically flexible and this enables real time communications (video as well as voice) to replicate the data model. To take just one example, the cost of relocating an employee on a traditional telephony network will cost around US $100; on a converged voice-data network there is no cost. Calls reach virtual locations in the same way as email.

Time for a pragmatic makeover

Profitability is the primary goal of commercial organizations. Profits increase if capital and operating expenditures can be reduced in ways that do not have a negative impact on the organization's ability to conduct its business, i.e. lower the service and support given to customers and prospects. Profits go up if productivity can be increased via better, more efficient ways of working. Superior services help retain customers and convert more prospects into customers, which results in better sales figures and improved profitability. These are business givens that no technology development should try and change.

At the height of the dot.com boom there were a number of systems that promised instant success. Many were purchased in haste; companies felt that they could not afford to fall behind in areas such as customer relationship management (CRM) and they are now looking to leverage those million dollar investments. In addition, there is a growing awareness of the limitations of stand-alone 'point solutions', despite the fact that they may be doing an adequate job and making a positive contribution towards the bottom line. Call centers, for example, were designed to handle telephony calls while Web sites used email as the primary communications medium. This indicates that the solution determines the way customers and prospects have to communicate with a business organization; it does not reflect the new expectation of the market, which is to communicate at any time using any media type.

These point solutions are hitting performance walls because of recent changes in the economic order, which is service centric. Callers have to define their requirements; press 1 for sales, 2 for support, etc; then they end up in a queue. Agents can only handle one telephone call at a time though they can juggle two to three email sessions, but email goes to Web sites, which were not designed to handle enquiries quickly and efficiently. Market research indicates that two thirds of email orders or inquiries receive no response. This figure demonstrates that stand-alone solutions are failing because the tasks that they were designed to perform have changed. Thus, we need a pragmatic makeover; pragmatic because of the need to protect legacy investments and enable a graceful transition to new 'holistic' solutions.

Stand-alone point solutions will not disappear overnight; instead their functionality will be retained and enhanced. Thus, there will be no disruption; work patterns will not change, they will become easier and more effective. Applications will interoperate without user intervention; one app will build on another to form a value chain, which users will be able to customize to meet their specific needs. In addition, there is a growing awareness of the need to make each component of the communications infrastructure aware of customers and their requirements. Customer-facing staff will therefore be able to customize a value chain that meets those needs.

This indicates that holistic solutions can be developed from bottom up and in future the implementation of modular applications that will not only be less rigid, but will also transition from processes that are focused inwards to those that are bi- and even multi-directional.

The new, networked economy is very demanding in its own right. Service expectations are high but delivery is complicated by the economic climate in which businesses currently operate. Thus, there is a Catch 22 situation. Companies that don't deliver will go out of business, but this time around management is not going to rush out and buy new systems. This indicates that the design of the new holistic solutions must recognize the need to leverage legacy investments in systems and infrastructures. However, despite recent problems in this sector, economic growth will come via advances in and widespread adoption of advanced networking technologies. The all-important difference is the fact that they will be deployed and employed in different ways to those of the recent past.

The cost of doing business

This book will detail the foundation upon which the new solutions are being created, indicate the innovative and productivity-enhancing applications, and suggest pragmatic migration strategies to take you from here to there. But let us put technology aside for the moment, since solutions are only means to an end. What are the key business issues that must be addressed? Can we encapsulate a plethora of performance and profitability issues and come up with a clearly defined point problem?

• Executive Summary

We can and the result is surprisingly simple. Businesses buy goods and services that they convert into other goods and/or services. That fundamental process involves numerous transactions and transaction costs represent that point problem. Professor Linda Garcia of Georgetown University defines transaction costs as *"the information-related costs of doing business."* She also states that these costs *"have a major impact on economic performance, the use of technology, and the structure and organization of firms. These costs have increased over time as markets have expanded and economic processes have become more complex."* [1]

That quote summarizes the problem and indicates that these costs are rising despite the best efforts of the information and communications community, but the implications are quite staggering when one sees the financial figures. Transaction costs are estimated to make up over half of the world's total GDP (gross domestic product) and the figure for 2000 was just over US $ 41 trillion. And there is no reason to suppose that a similar percentage figure does not apply to the cost of doing business.

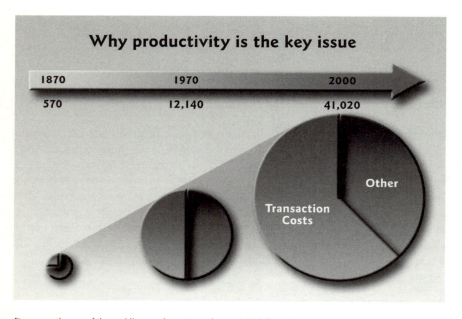

Figures are the sum of the world's gross domestic products in US$ billions. Source: Bradford DeLong, Wallis/North.

[1] D. Linda Garcia, Governing Electronic Commerce in a Global Environment, East-West Center Working Papers, economic series no. 31, August 2001.

'Information related' is a broad term; it encompasses accessing and disseminating information; collaboration and coordination as well as consulting, selling, billing and so on. This indicates the importance of information and communications technology and the need for it to be applied in a way that will halt and then reverse the rate at which this cost is rising.

The statement that economic processes have become more complex is self-evident. This has resulted in work becoming more specialized, which means that more people are involved in day-to-day business decisions. A team of financial experts, for example, will typically support the CEO. This is acceptable as long as the benefits of specialization outweigh the increased communications and collaboration overhead. When the reverse is true, specialists will be deployed at the local level, where they are close to the customers. These are basic assumptions of the current economic system.

The only way out of this financial circle is to retain the benefits of specialization but employ more effective and efficient communications and collaboration technology in order to drive down costs. If one can deploy solutions that come close to replicating one-on-one meetings then those specialist skills can be leveraged, i.e. they can be spread around the organization. This means that fewer specialists are needed since the resource they represent can be shared. Put another way, improved productivity is achieved via better communications.

Transaction costs are also rising because workforces have become more mobile; they are closer to the customer (physically), but there is a downside since absence from the office makes it harder to communicate and collaborate effectively. In addition, there is a disconnect between a mobile salesperson and the back office information he/she needs, e.g. prices, delivery dates, etc. Setting up a secure data connection is not easy, but it is impossible if the workforce is relying on cellular phones. Companies have made significant investments in back office systems such as CRM in order to lower transaction costs, but the access door is shut when employees are mobile.

Messaging, which comes in different media flavors, seeks to address the issue of communications and collaboration; however this is a point solution that has hit a productivity wall. Research indicates that employees now spend an average of 2.5 hours a day accessing and processing their email, voicemail and fax messages. This is a surprisingly high figure, but a study published by the Wall Street Journal found that the average employee sends and receives more than 200 messages a day. Thus, messaging in general and voicemail in particular has become a significant part of the problem.

There is an intrinsic need for people to communicate in real time and this can actually reduce productivity since it results in 'call me back' voicemails being left on different systems by both parties. In addition, there may be similar 'I really need to talk to you' requests being sent via email and the new instant messaging systems. Failure to connect therefore becomes a hidden cost; hidden because it is hard to quantify, but messaging back and forth instead of connecting and communicating clearly wastes a lot of time and employee time is money.

• Executive Summary

Too many messages and inefficient business processes represent a very significant transaction cost and if more than half the world's GDP is based on these costs, it does not require a great cognitive leap to realize that a similar percentage figure applies to the typical enterprise. It will vary from industry to industry and company to company, but it does represent a substantial part of the cost of doing business. And it is also clear that productivity is the key issue: it is the area where the biggest gains can be realized.

IP convergence

IP convergence enables lower operating costs, better communications, improved productivity and superior service offers. The hype is over, now it's happening and early adopters are realizing these significant benefits. However, for historic reasons misunderstandings about this groundbreaking development still prevail. For example, the transmission of voice traffic over an IP network (VoIP) is simply a transportation mechanism. There is an analogy to mains electricity; it only becomes useful when it drives an appliance. VoIP is employed so that voice (and video) traffic can employ the same communications protocol (IP) as data traffic, enabling everything to run over the same network. This reduces communications and network management costs, but the biggest benefit — the electrical appliances — comes via the applications. In addition we have the intrinsic flexibility of IP, which allows services and applications to be hosted anywhere on the corporate network and to be accessed by all authorized users, regardless of their location.

IP convergence therefore brings together the formerly disparate worlds of voice and data and enables a best-of-both-worlds environment to be deployed. A key issue was the quality of service (QoS) of telephony when transmitted as a stream of data packets. Voice is a real time medium that is influenced by transmission delays and variations in delay; however, QoS mechanisms that prioritize voice and video traffic have been developed. Thus, this issue has been resolved and call quality over a managed IP network is normally at least as good as that of the public network and quite often it is superior.

The way ahead

Having concluded that transaction costs and productivity are the two main concerns, let us try and do the same thing for holistic solutions.

The need to integrate information (data) and real time communications (voice) is a given. In an information-centric economy the use of two incompatible networks only makes sense from a historic perspective. Voice-data convergence has been an industry-wide mantra for a decade or more and many enterprises have transitioned or are transitioning to a single network. The debates about reliability, quality of service and other important issues are over; now it's a question of when and how, not if.

Executive Summary •

Convergence is the all-important first step and one that allows communications costs to be significantly reduced. For example, the corporate VPN is used for voice as well as data, thereby eliminating the need for expensive leased lines. The next involves the *addition* of second-generation, IP-centric platforms to the new infrastructure. Addition was italicized to emphasize that convergence does not imply automatic and immediate replacement of PBXs, which this book defines as first-generation telephony platforms. The new platforms run the new applications and productivity-enhancing applications are the driving force behind this development. This second step also facilitates interoperation between real time telephony and data-centric business processes.

The experience of end users is that of a seamless interface and it is created via computer telephony software. However, a genuine holistic solution will ultimately be based on converged voice-data platforms, i.e. enterprise servers that host mainstream business processes; handle email, instant messaging and voicemail; and have *embedded real time telephony functionality*. This third-generation development will elevate the functionality of the network by enabling real time communications to become a component of Microsoft's upcoming .Net data landscape. However, it is worth noting that there is no need to wait. Second-generation platforms are delivering innovative productivity-enhancing applications today (see Chapter 2) and they have to be in place in order for the functionality to be elevated.

Holistic solutions will therefore be based on a converged network that handles all media types and real time platforms that process all media types as well as the more traditional computer server tasks. Similar real time operating systems will run on the client side of the client-server model and these are already being employed, e.g. Windows XP. This operating system also incorporates Windows Messenger, which is an Instant Messaging (IM) application. However, it can be linked to other media types such as voice and video and be used to facilitate data sharing. (Earlier operating systems can be upgraded to support certain aspects of this IM application). IBM has a similar real time application known as Sametime.

This business graphic, which comes from Deloitte Consulting Research, indicates the growing importance of these new IP-enabled communications applications. It also shows that once convergence has been achieved there is no increase in the value of the supporting infrastructure.

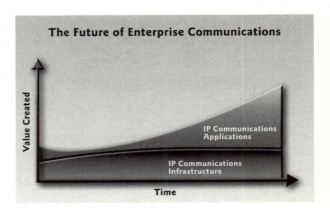

• Executive Summary

On the server side of the client-server model Microsoft is developing a new operating system component called Greenwich. This component, formally known as RTC (Real Time Communications), will be an integrated part of .Net server. Thus, Greenwich plus .Net form the basis of a new real time operating system from Microsoft. Greenwich will facilitate real time communications via a set of baseline telephony functions, but these will be enhanced via software extensions. This is software that functions as a 'communications broker' and it will come from the telecommunications industry. This is a necessary and logical development since real time telephony encompasses several hundred functions and features plus a century of operating experience.

These developments are enabling phones and PCs to complement each other; in fact, integration between these devices is so tight that they effectively function as one. For example, IM is normally used to indicate online data presence; are colleagues logged onto the network or not. A flag on the PC's screen shows green for presence and red for absence. Real time integration allows similar telephony flags to indicate if colleagues are free to talk or not. If the IM flag is green then they are on the network and can be reached, but if the telephone flag is red then they are talking. This simple, but remarkably effective application saves time by eliminating telephony tag, i.e. parties leaving voicemails for each other and failing to connect. If the call is urgent and the other party is talking then an instant message can be sent and a reply such as 'I'll call you right back' sent while the party continues to talk.

That was just one example of the new applications that are going to boost productivity and minimize transaction costs.

This four-layer model represents the new holistic solution. A converged network is easier and cheaper to manage than two; thus opex is lower and an ROI is delivered. ROIs are also generated at the other three layers, but it is the applications that boost productivity and thereby minimize transaction costs. In addition, the relevant IP-enhanced applications are customer-focused, which allows companies to deliver superior services to those of the competition.

Leading companies from the information and communications industry support the concept, but this should not be seen as an example of jam tomorrow but no jam today. Very significant boosts in productivity are realized after the transition to a converged infrastructure and the introduction of second-generation platforms and the all-important IP-enhanced applications. Thus, IP convergence is not a development that can be put on the back burner.

• 18

Getting from here to there

As indicated earlier, traditional voice networks and data networks are disparate: they employ different communications technologies and have radically different architectures. Telephony is a rich, real time media that is sensitive to delays and the architecture is centralized; PBXs sit on the company's premises and each site has to have its own switching facility. Data is not time sensitive; the architecture is flexible and distributed; the physical location of services and applications is not relevant and all authorized users can employ them, i.e. their location is also irrelevant. This indicates that the new converged infrastructure has to be carefully planned and engineered so that there is no perceived difference in the quality of the calls and that all the requisite telephony functionality is retained.

One can make a valid, stand-alone business case for the transition to a single, converged network but the lower operating costs that result are not the raison d'être for IP-centric communications. Productivity enhancing applications, particularly real time applications, are the driving force.

These applications run on one or more computer servers and they are 'managed' by IP platforms. Their functionality is similar to that of a regular PBX, hence the term 'IP PBX', however in some ways this is a confusing designation. At first sight one might think that the PBXs have to be replaced by the new platforms in order to realize the benefits, but this is not the case. One or more platforms have to be added to the network as well as new IP phones, but there is no need to 'rip and replace' legacy hardware. Companies have invested around $250 billion in PBX systems; that is an estimate of the world's installed base and this figure clearly indicates that migrating to the new IP platforms is a process that needs to be and will be considered very carefully. However, in a green-field site situation where there is no legacy PBX there is no issue: it really is that simple. So if you are adding a new location to your corporate network this is a great way to evaluate those benefits.

Concerns about the so-called Millennium bug resulted in a sales surge of PBXs at the end of the '90s so a significant percentage of that base is new and if these first-generation systems are working well, which they are, it's difficult (make that impossible) to justify replacing them with IP platforms. At the same time, businesses cannot afford to ignore the considerable benefits of IP enhanced applications and their positive impact on transaction costs and productivity.

The first migration step is issue free. Regular PBXs can be IP enabled via VoIP (Voice over IP) gateways. This allows virtual private network (VPN) services to replace the expensive leased lines used to create private networks. Operating expenses are much lower; transparent dialing and the other features of private networks are retained. In addition, the full functionality of the PBX can now be extended to small sites. A VPN service can also be shared with customers and suppliers, thereby leveraging the value of the new infrastructure. Value-added services can also be employed.

• Executive Summary

The second step involves the introduction of IP platforms. There are two basic categories: converged platforms that enable both regular and IP-enhanced telephony, and native IP platforms that only enable IP telephony. The latter would be used in green field sites. Converged platforms provide full connectivity to IP-based devices and to other converged PBXs via IP. Users who need the new communications functionality require new IP phones and/or softphones (PCs and PDAs that run IP communications software). Over time more phones can be added and eventually the new platforms take over from the PBXs. A key benefit is the retention of legacy phones and the cabling, i.e. nothing changes for users whose needs are adequately served by regular telephony. Native IP platforms can also be connected to PBXs, but in this case an external VoIP gateway is employed, and when the PBX is retired the regular phones have to be replaced. Migration scenarios might also involve a mix of converged and pure IP platforms.

In a post-migration scenario IT platforms running databases, CRM systems, email, etc., are on the same network as the new, converged telephony platforms. Thus, what were previously isolated back office systems can now be brought into a single, unified, real time workflow. And customized communications portals, which are covered in this section, extend that unified user experience to mobile workforces. Thus, the door to corporate and personal information stays open when employees leave the office.

Maximizing productivity while minimizing stress

People who operate in the new economy are already stretched so we need to find ways of working better instead of simply asking them to work even harder. There are limits and when stretched too far productivity actually declines and staff burn out. Key staff may also leave if expectations are set too high.

In order to demonstrate how communicating applications can square the productivity/stress circle let us consider telephone tag. This term is used to describe the process whereby John calls Julie and gets her voicemail. He leaves a 'please call me back' message. Julie calls back and gets John's voice mail. She tells him that 'I called you back but you were busy'. If John and Julie are busy people getting in touch may take some time, and if the reason for calling is urgent the delay could be serious. If it is urgent then John may ring Julie's mobile number and there's a good chance that he'll get voicemail again, but this time on a second system. John may also decide to send an SMS, and since he has no way of knowing if Julie's mobile is busy or not switched on, he might also send an email and/or an instant message. Eventually Julie will call back, after listening to different voicemails on different systems and reading emails and instant messages.

This is an everyday scenario. It's frustrating and stressful; it wastes a lot time and time is money. Now we can see why transaction costs are so high and why they continue to rise.

Earlier we mentioned the increase in specialization, which means that more people need to collaborate in order to reach a decision. So imagine that John needs to set up an unscheduled conference call with Mary and Alan as well as Julie. Now the everyday scenario is about to become a communications nightmare. Multiple messages asking everybody to be free at a certain time would need to be sent to multiple devices and even then there is no guarantee that all parties would participate. Life was much easier when work represented a place and the phone on the desktop was the only way to communicate, but we've moved on to a more complex environment and invented too many point solutions along the way.

We have more than enough technology: virtual personal assistants that try and find you; email, SMS, and instant messages. We also have a more than adequate supply of devices: wireline and wireless phones, PCs and PDAs. And that is the problem. They are not joined up; what is clearly needed is a way of managing one's availability.

Presence and availability

Let's replay the John-Julie scenario but this time we include some communications smarts: deliverable smarts. John and Julie have set up 'buddy lists' on their PCs in order to exchange instant messages with their colleagues. When a buddy is on line a small icon appears on the screen of the PC and this allows two or more parties to start 'chatting'. The terms buddy and chat indicate that instant messaging (IM) started out as an Internet application.

IP telephony enables tight integration of PCs and phones, so a little bit of computer telephony software allows the same icon to show the phone's status on PC screens. If Julie is in the office but on the phone her telephony presence will be displayed in John's buddy list, so he doesn't call her until she comes off the line. The icon would typically be green when available and red when not, so John can make easy checks from time to time.

That is a very simple application, but it meets a very real need. Secure IM is becoming a very popular communications medium; it's not intrusive; it's quicker and easier to handle than email; and more and more communications smarts are being developed. For example, two or more parties may start a chat session and then decide that it would be easier to talk. This can be done via a couple of mouse clicks. The application knows who is chatting and it knows their numbers, so setting up additional media types such as telephony and eventually video is a breeze.

IM can also be used to set up conference calls. The application detects the presence and availability of all parties and as soon as everybody is free to talk the phones start ringing. The presence and availability of mobile phones is always known to the network; without it the service could not function and this information can be used by the same application. This is a particularly valuable bonus but it does require a business agreement between the enterprise and its mobile network operator. On one hand it does represent a revenue loss for

• Executive Summary

operators since calls made to mobile phones that are busy result in voicemail and returned calls. On the other hand it is a very good way of cementing the business relationship and in minimizing the loss of a large customer to another operator. Time will tell how mobile presence works out in the marketplace, but operators are unlikely to ignore the longer-term potential of this and other value-added services.

Managed availability

So far so good; presence and availability boost productivity, minimize frustration and stress, and make a significant impact on transaction costs, but it gets better. Telephony is a rich communications medium; the human voice is the best way to convey subtle messages, to express feelings and emotions; it is also the optimal way to reach consensus on tricky issues. But this communications medium is intrusive; phones ring and even if the ID of the calling party is displayed and the call diverted to voicemail, the called party has been disturbed. In addition, unwanted calls can get through. Thus, in addition to making one's presence and availability known to the system, users need to define when they are available and to whom. This is how it works on one particular solution.

Users only give out a single virtual phone number. They create a contact list on their PC and give specific instructions as to the options that should be offered to these callers. For example: my partner and my boss can reach me at all times. Customers should be connected to my mobile phone when I am away from the office. When I am in a meeting they should be informed and told when I will be free to return the call. Suppliers should be diverted to voicemail but given the option of sending an instant message when I am in the office and an SMS when I am mobile. Setting up these management parameters does require some thought and effort, but it is basically a one-time process that saves massive amounts of time later on. And as buddies come and go it is easy to add, delete and fine-tune these availability parameters.

The solution presents the relevant options to the caller when that virtual number is called. This makes it much easier for callers on the contact list and gives users more control over disruptive interruptions. It also minimizes having the same message left on different services.

Let us consider a hypothetical example of managed availability. David has defined these communications options for Kim: leave a message, schedule a meeting, dictate an email or send an instant message to my PDA. This user has not authorized mobile/cellular calls from Kim, nor has the number been given out. Access to confidential information such as David's agenda is secured using voiceprint authentication. When Kim calls, the system tells David that Kim is on the line by sending an instant message to his voice-enabled PDA. David can then take Kim out of this automated transaction and talk to her using his device of choice.

David and Kim decide to meet on Tuesday, not Thursday. If David is mobile he simply tells the system to access his calendar and then schedules the meeting using spoken commands. This indicates how IP-enabled voice becomes an integral part of the information infrastructure. David could also tap a time slot on his PDA's calendar. Once scheduled, the solution could also reserve a meeting room or accommodate other user preferences. Other parties can also be invited to the meeting. The groupware calendar functions create an invitation and the user then dictates the subject and message.

In addition, users can leave different information for different callers by recording the message in the voicemail system or by placing it on a Web page. The transition to an all-IP information and communications environment means that multi-modal[2] devices can be transferred from the voice system directly to a Web page in order to view or download additional information such as a document, spreadsheet or presentation.

Managed availability is not a new concept and various attempts were made in the past to provide similar functionality, but they failed due to the intrinsic problem of getting the disparate worlds of telephony and computing to work with each other. Replicating the phone on a PC did not make sense, particularly when the functionality was limited and the interface clumsy, but everything changes when there is a converged environment that uses the same communications protocol (IP). This does enable 100% replication, but that is not the primary objective. The phone is what we expect to use for telephony, but its computing and other resources are limited. The PC can therefore complement the phone in many ways, one of which was the seamless integration of instant messaging with presence. It is also used to enable point and click telephony from address books and to set up conference calls simply by dragging and dropping names.

Media types and their usage

In recent years we have seen email traffic grow at an incredible rate. This media type is convenient, virtually free, non-intrusive, can carry attachments and is ideal for collaborating across time zones. Unfortunately it has become too convenient, e.g. business professionals are receiving up to 200 messages a day. Instant messaging is a more recent development, particularly in the corporate environment, is taking off at an even more incredible rate and this media type, which is close to near time, is taking its place on desktop PCs. So where does this leave voice? The statistics indicate a lowly 7% p.a. growth but this figure is misleading. IP communications puts telephony back onto its original center stage position and, voice followed by video, will become very important, 21st century media types. However, what is important is not the respective merits of one way of communicating over another,

---

[2]) *The term multi-modal indicates the ability to function in more than one mode of operation, e.g. to perform both as a voice and data device.*

• Executive Summary

but the fact that communications barriers such as cost are being removed and brand-new communications processes are being developed and deployed.

Step back and reflect

The potential of automated presence and managed availability is enormous. This application is too new to be quantified, but common sense tells us that the ability to communicate and collaborate easily and quickly will make an immediate and significant impact on transaction costs. On the client side we have the requisite operating system; on the server side we have second-generation platforms, so there is no need to wait.

Less obvious is the fact that there is a seamless and synergistic relationship between different stand-alone applications. IM is a valuable communications tool in its own right and usage in corporations is rising. There are early indications that it is already reducing the number of business emails. IM indicates (data) presence on the network but convergence enables a tight link to availability. The same buddy list window shows telephone icons that indicate whether colleagues are available to talk or not. In turn availability is managed via the PC and can be linked to personal agendas. Thus, one application builds on another; there is no need to reinvent communications wheels. In future this concept will be advanced via software components that are used in totally different applications.

These developments indicate that all the talk about the information-age economy is somewhat misplaced. Information per se is just the raw material; it is the automation of information processing that will boost productivity and lower transaction costs. And as in the industrial age, automation will also remove much of the drudgery and stress, e.g. deleting unwanted emails and handling too many messages.

Unified messaging and unified communications

The power of today's networks lies in their ability to allow people to communicate quickly, even instantly, using various mechanisms. It is hard to imagine how an organization would function without voice mail, email, and facsimile, but there is a downside, as we have seen. Too much time is spent accessing and processing messages and the problem is particularly acute for mobile workers. Downloading everything is costly and time consuming, particularly over a cellular telephony network, and it can only be done to a mobile data device. But important messages have to be read and processed; even a short delay may antagonize an important customer.

The particular needs of mobile workforces are met via a unified approach to communications. This is a very broad subject and different vendors use different definitions of unified

Executive Summary

communications, but everybody agrees that you start by enabling real time access to a unified inbox.

Unified Messaging (UM) is not a new concept, but this application did not reach many corporate desktops despite its ability to increase employee productivity significantly. This came from the fact that voice and data occupied disparate environments, which meant that the integration and network management cost overshadowed the benefits. A converged network, however, provides the necessary platform for this application.

The ability to view and process all message types in a single inbox brings significant productivity and convenience benefits. Having everything in one place instead of two means that important voicemails are not missed and others can be listened to later or deleted. Voicemail and faxes can also be forwarded to other parties and be sorted using the same criteria as email.

This indicates that the increase in productivity comes via time saved, which is considerable. A study from Comgroup found that office workers experienced a 53% time-saving when using UM and the figure was 70% for mobile users. Another study by The Radicati Group found that this application generated 25 to 40 minutes of additional productivity per employee per day and reduced IT support and administrative costs up to 70 percent.

The basic idea behind Unified Communications (UC) is to allow messages that are in the unified inbox to be processed via voice commands. Thus, this application is ideal for mobile workers whose only mobile device is a phone. For example, they can listen to new messages when on the move using simple commands like next, delete and reply. Replies can be dictated to the system, which sends voicemail attachments to the senders. This can be done several times a day, so the inbox does not build up, and the really important messages are heard in time. In the case of salespeople, this convenient communications capability can be used to keep customers satisfied, to react quickly to sales leads and generally be more productive. Executives and managers can use a hands-free mobile/cellular phone in the car and listen to messages on their way to work. Thus, even the time spent sitting in traffic jams can become productive.

Solutions that have additional functionality are coming to the marketplace. These will list missed calls and log outbound calls. They will also enable the mobile user to tell the system to call the sender of an email, i.e. there is no need to dial the number if details of the calling party are known, which will be the case for colleagues and other designated parties. However, the combination of UC, IM, Presence and Managed Availability will solve a large part of the messaging problem at source.

• Executive Summary

Softphones

IP Telephony software is available for desktop or notebook PCs, which explains the term softphone. This means that users of notebooks can take their extension with them and can make and receive calls from any location on the corporate network. The functionality is equivalent to having all the telephony features of a regular IP phone on a computer. Similar functionality can be enabled on Pocket PC PDAs. An IP softphone also simplifies the provisioning of multimedia contact center agents capable of handling voice calls, emails and interactive Web calls. Softphones are therefore an ideal complement to a desktop device and they can present the same information in different ways to suit the individual needs of the user.

The screen size of some IP phones is similar to that of a PDA and in many ways these devices resemble a small computer. This means that they can be employed as thin-client devices in client-server data environments. They employ menu-driven graphical interfaces and other PC-type features such as the ability to search the corporate directory and set up personal directories. In addition, IP phones will normally have flash memory in order to facilitate software upgrades.

Communications portals

Portals are a well-established concept on the Internet, but enterprise class communications portals are relatively new. They reflect the near ubiquitous use of the intuitive browser interface as well as the tight integration of voice and data. The basic idea is to provide a common point of access to all authorized communications services and applications that the user requires. This will typically comprise the unified inbox, personal and group agendas and selected host resources, e.g. price and delivery data of the products that make up a salesperson's portfolio.

The functionality of these portals includes device mediation, media translation and secure access via a single logon. Device mediation is used to provide the appropriate communications features to the user's device, i.e. the system recognizes the difference between the resources of a PDA and a phone. Media translation includes speech to text and text to voice. This is needed for unified communications. The single logon enables access to all network-based functions — basic telephony features, one number office/cellular access, and enterprise applications that employ embedded communications functions.

Individuals and enterprises can create simple or complex voice portal applications using standard Web authoring tools and templates for regular call processing applications. Portals can also be customized. Thus, everybody in the organization can have fast, easy access to the information and services they need. A salesman, for example, can go directly to the relevant part of a database using a cellular phone and listen to price and delivery information.

Unified messaging, unified communications and communications portals are therefore a set of tightly linked applications.

Conclusions

This section has highlighted the importance of IP communications and demonstrated the impact of innovative communications applications on personal productivity and transaction costs. Big claims were made for these developments; justifications come in the following chapters together with details on more applications and related topics, e.g. the ability to communications enable mainstream applications such as CRM and a growing recognition that the corporate network is a source of competitive advantage.

Exactly how and when your organization will take IP Communications on board will depend on many factors, the most important being the need to protect legacy investments in PBXs, phones and cabling. But it is only a question of time, direction, and individual requirements.

Real time communications, video as well as voice, is following the open systems/standards route of the PC as well as the more recent Web model and the implications for the industry are seismic. Hardware will become a commodity; functionality, applications and support services will become the core competences of the communications industry.

CHAPTER ONE
Issues and explanations

This chapter covers the difference between regular telephony and that of IP telephony and the issues that arise when planning and making the transition. The intrinsic flexibility of the new medium is explained as well as the new communications concepts that it enables. The chapter concludes with a short explanation of new real time voice-data platforms.

At first sight the key benefits given in the previous sections might seem to be too good to be true. If this development can cut costs, boost productivity and hone competitive edges then surely IP Communications should be at the forefront of every corporate agenda and there would be no need for this book. So why is this not the case?

Regular telephony employs circuit switching. Public and private switches (PBXs) establish end-to-end circuits that are used for the duration of the call.

Legacy systems are a key issue. Companies have invested around $250 billion in PBX hardware; that is an estimate of the world's installed base and this figure clearly indicates that migrating to the new IP platforms is a process that needs to be and will be considered very carefully. Concerns about the so-called Millennium bug resulted in a sales surge at the end of the '90s so a significant percentage of that base is new and if these PBXs are working well, which they are, it's difficult (make that impossible) to justify replacing them with IP platforms.

Packet switching is used in IP Communications. In this case the circuit is virtual, not physical. Signals are sent as a stream of small packets.

PBXs are being replaced with IP platforms when they come to the end of their life cycles, but in many situations managers are still looking at ways of protecting the not inconsiderable investment in phones and telephony cabling. This can be done using 'IP converged' platforms. The term indicates that both circuit and packet switching are employed in the same system and in many locations these communications platforms represent an optimal, low-entry point

• Issues and explanations

solution. Employees who do not need the additional functionality that is enabled by IP Communications continue with their regular phones; the remainder gets new IP phones and/or softphones. This is also an excellent way to evaluate the benefits and ensure that the network is adequately provisioned for the new traffic. Thus, one location can migrate in this way before upgrading the remainder of the infrastructure.

In a green-field site situation where there is no legacy PBX, there is no issue: it's that simple. So if you are adding a new location to your corporate network this is an alternative way of evaluating those benefits. But in most other situations the migration process is more complex and this important issue is covered in Chapter 3.

Protecting legacy investments is an important issue, but uncertainty about the concept prevails in some quarters, which is unfortunate. IP Telephony is not the same thing as Internet Telephony, but the similarity between these two terms is confusing. This is another reason why this book refers to IP Communications, but the 'I' in IP remains that of the Internet. The confusion between the Internet and Internet protocols and standards is therefore understandable. IP Telephony, which should be seen as a sub-set of IP Communications, involves real time communications that meets stringent QoS requirements, i.e. it is at least as good as the public network. The requisite QoS is enabled on the organization's LANs and/or across a WAN where there is a Service Level Agreement (SLA) between the organization and the service provider. Nevertheless VoIP continues to have negative overtones for historic reasons, an issue that is addressed in this section.

QoS (Quality of Service) is the key VoIP issue. This is a broad term used to describe mechanisms that (a) detect that the data packets are those of a real time medium (voice or video) and (b) that route the packets according to their priority.

Before proceeding, we should point out that sales of IP Communications systems are very healthy, particularly when one considers the hit taken by the economy after collapses in the dotcom and teledotcom sectors. The market was estimated to be worth US$ 44 Billion in 2002 rising to US$ 50 Billion in 2004. Note that sales only started in earnest in 2000 because of earlier concerns about the Millennium bug. However, analysts predict that sales of the new communications platforms will equal those of PBXs around 2005/6 and after that date they surge ahead.

VoIP enables voice and data applications to be distributed over the same network together with remote data access.

Research conducted in 2001 by Dynamic Markets contained some interesting findings. For example, 77% of large- and medium-sized companies did not understand the term VoIP fully and many did not even recognize it. On the other hand, 90% of early adopters were positive about their use of the IP Telephony systems; 48% were very positive and none were negative. However, 66% of the companies questioned had no plans to adopt IP Telephony for these reasons: initial investment too high (19%); no additional benefits (15%); lack of supporting infrastructure (14%); lack of clear information on benefits (12%).

These statistics indicate that adopters are either positive or very positive about the benefits, yet at the same time the figures underline the uncertainty factor. A key objective of this book is to communicate the former and remove the latter.

How does regular telephony work?

A basic appreciation of the difference between circuit-switched and packet-switched telephony is needed in order to see how the key benefits are realized and understand why a degree of confusion about VoIP prevails. No technical knowledge is required to understand these sections.

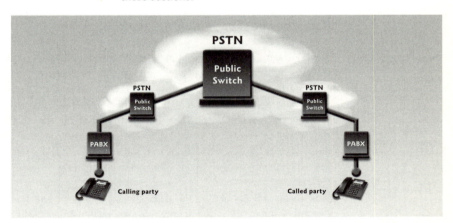

Figure 1.1: *Calls between two parties are set up by a series of private and public switches. The resulting communications link is retained for the duration of the call, which explains why tariffs are also based on time.*

Switches interconnect to each other via circuits and a circuit has to be established before two parties can talk to each other. Switching is performed by exchanges in the public network; in the US they are called central office switches. PBXs in organizations perform the

• Issues and explanations

same function; a PBX is a Private Branch eXchange. Figure 1.1 shows how calls are set up.

The public network is known as the PSTN (Public Service Telephony Network)

A PBX in one office might switch the call to a local exchange, which then switches it to a national exchange, from there it might go to an international exchange, and then proceed back down the link until it reaches another PBX and the called party. This explains why tariffs are based on distance.

PBXs switch calls from phones to and from the PSTN (public switched telephony network); they also handle internal calls.

The majority of the PSTN has been digitized. However, most of the final connections to homes (the so-called last mile) are analog. Digital 'last mile' connections are known as ISDN (Integrated Services Digital network) lines.

The baseline circuit-switched technology stretches all the way back to the 19th century and it is connection-oriented, i.e. a pre-defined path is set up through the network. Each switch operates independently but they all act in concert. Once the connection is established it is maintained on an exclusive, continuous basis until the call is terminated. The end-to-end resource cannot be shared. This indicates that the technology is not particularly efficient, but it is perfect for real time voice and video traffic.

How does packet switching work?

The packets that TCP/IP routes contain the destination address and the destination network. Thus, messages can be sent to multiple networks. This is known as multicasting, i.e. information is sent to specific groups.

The PSTN was designed for real time communications. IP Telephony, however, is based on Internet technology and the Internet was designed to handle data traffic. The Net grew out of a US military infrastructure that had one very special requirement: it was literally designed to be bomb proof. Thus, before looking at the way that VoIP works on corporate networks, you need to know something about the task for which IP was created and why the needs of voice and data communications are so fundamentally different.

To be technically correct we should be looking at TCP/IP, which is a protocol suite. TCP is the acronym for the related Transmission Control Protocol, but IP is the foundation. IP defines the size of the packets and the address information they carry.

X.25 and Frame Relay are packet-switched technologies that pre-date IP. Both continue to be employed, e.g. X.25 is used to make credit card checks.

Packet switching started a century later than circuit switching. As shown in figure 1.2, instead of transmitting data as a continuous stream of bits (the circuit switched way) the file is chopped up into small packets. The address information tells the packets where to go and when they are 'launched' into the network they find their own way. Packet switching is therefore connectionless. Thus, if the direct communications link between Washington and Los Angeles went down then traffic would travel by an alternative route and still get through. That was the military angle.

In addition to government agencies, the network was used to link universities and similar academic institutions in order to exchange research information. This process was facilitated by the fact that TCP/IP was designed to enable communications between disparate networks, computer hardware, operating systems and transmission media. That is why this protocol suite is mandated for use on the Internet and why it has become the lingua franca of data communications.

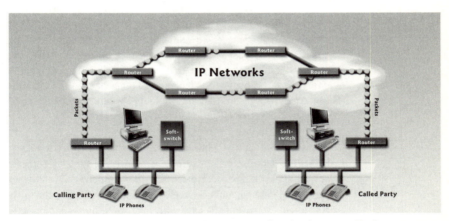

Figure 1.2.: *Calls between two parties are established by routing a flow of packets over an IP infrastructure. The telephony server identifies each packet, i.e. the address to which it is sent and its sequence.*

The first priority in the PSTN is to ensure uptime. The first priority in IP networks is to avoid loss of packets. Real time communications over IP is therefore a paradigm shift since the priorities of the network are reversed.

Unless there is congestion or a broken link, IP packets will take a direct route through the network. The packets carry the address of the recipient computer and these addresses are read at high speed by routers, which are specialized computers having routing tables that are constantly updated. After reading the address the router decides on the most expedient route for the next leg of the journey. This process takes less than a millisecond but delays can build up and they can also be variable since packets may travel by different routes.

TCP is used to set up a virtual connection through IP networks. It gives each packet a sequence number and adds an error control mechanism. At the receiving end TCP takes control and ensures that

• Issues and explanations

the packets are assembled in the right order and if any are lost or corrupted the relevant packets are retransmitted and inserted into the right place in the file.

Note that IP is not concerned with the contents of a data file: it can be a Word document, a PowerPoint presentation or a set of database records. It can also be a voice or video signal that has been digitized and packetized.

Packet switching is more efficient than circuit switching. Communications resources are shared and tariffs are based on the amount of data transmitted, not duration and distance. Thus, there is no charge when there is a pause in the conversation, even when it is measured in milliseconds. A pause in the conversation releases a resource that can be used for another call (the system introduces a pause of the same length at the receiving end). In addition, VoIP signals can be compressed in order to allow more calls to be carried. Network managers can use this feature to minimize bandwidth requirements or maximize call quality on an individual office or even an individual user basis. This means that three to four calls can be accommodated using an equivalent circuit-switched network resource.

It is worth noting that while packetized voice is sensitive to delays, packetized data, e.g. emails, are not. If messages arrive a few seconds or minutes late it does not matter. On the other hand each and every packet of a data file must be received; if one packet is lost the file is corrupted. This is not the case with telephony; our hearing is able to bridge gaps in conversations and small gaps such as the loss of a few packets have no impact on the perceived quality of the call.

VoIP issues

Latency *is the average time it takes for a packet to travel from the source to the destination.*

In regular telephony speech signals are digitized; this is done by sampling the amplitude of the signal 8000 times a second. Thus, each digital element is separated in time by 125 milliseconds and this timing relationship must be maintained across the network. That is why voice is known as a synchronous medium. This means that latency (delay) must be minimal and jitter (variations in delay) should be close to zero. This is accomplished by giving each call a dedicated circuit having more than enough bandwidth.

Issues and explanations

Packet data works perfectly over voice networks but the reverse is not true. Every router introduces a delay and if it builds up to around 300 milliseconds an echo effect is experienced and at 500 milliseconds the quality of the call is not acceptable for business purposes. This would seem to indicate that VoIP is a non-starter and even if engineers could get it to work, why bother?

It is ironic that a network designed for voice (the PSTN) was made to work for data. More recently a network designed for data (the Internet) is being re-engineered to handle telephony.

Why bother is covered in the next section. VoIP on the Internet was close to being a non-starter in 1994 when VocalTec started marketing PC-to-PC software. (The concept was first demonstrated back in 1964.) Delays built up due to insufficient bandwidth and the relatively low routing speed and at times there were breaks in transmission.

The word hype does not do justice to the early days of Internet Telephony. The media predicated the rapid demise of the incumbent carriers and then people started using VoIP software. However, call quality was very poor and could not be used for business communications. The media then trashed the concept. And today, even when the difference between Internet and IP Telephony is understood, when VoIP is demonstrated on a well-provisioned, managed network, call quality being at least as good as that of the PSTN, the key benefit is still thought to be cost for that historic reason. It was at the time, but carriers were always able to compete on price and large organizations having equally large telephony bills were able to negotiate good deals.

Internet Telephony therefore got a bad reception and unfortunately the association with today's VoIP technology lingers on in some quarters. However, although LANs and WANs use IP for data communications, they do not form part of the Internet so you can forget the past. Bandwidth has become a commodity and routers now function at blinding speeds; moreover mechanisms now exist that give priority to voice traffic. This means that call quality is at least as good as that of the PSTN and on a well-managed network it may even be superior.

Incumbent carriers (former PTTs) are migrating their network cores in order to handle IP traffic and be able to offer managed network services .

Why be concerned with problems of the past? One reason was the need to explain the difference between IP Telephony and Internet Telephony. Another was to generate awareness of the need to ensure that your LANs have been engineered for VoIP in advance and that the service on which your WAN depends is up to the task.

• Issues and explanations

These are not significant issues but they do need to be taken into consideration.

Why bother?

The cost of reallocating a telephone extension is variously estimated to lie between US$75 and 125. In some companies around 20% of the workforce need to be reassigned every year.

The fact that VoIP can deliver quality telephony over private IP networks means that one infrastructure can be used for voice as well as data. That brings cost savings, particularly on the network management side, but it does not add up to a compelling business case. That comes via this key benefit:

> *"The ease with which communications applications are employed and the speed with which new applications are created and implemented. New functionality can be added in virtually the same way as new plug-ins for Web browsers."*

CTI was long on promise and short on delivery because the cost of integration exceeded the value of the new functionality. Thus, valid concepts such as unified messaging were not widely implemented.

When voice has been digitized computers can process the signals. Telephony devices can then be used in the client-server model. When voice uses the same communications protocol as computer data, applications can interoperate seamlessly with business processes. In addition, employees can move around the network, logon from any location and their phone calls will follow them in the same way as email. Thus, hot desking is an intrinsic feature; it's free and the cost of telephony adds, moves and changes is eliminated. Finally, telephony can profit from other Internet technologies such as the Web and dynamic addressing. This indicates that VoIP is rapidly becoming a killer service. Reasons enough one would think.

Computer Telephony Integration (CTI)

There is nothing new about the idea of harnessing computing power in order to advance the functionality of phones and the public telephony infrastructure. The problem lay in the complexity and therefore the cost of integrating the world of voice with the world of data. As long as these two media types occupied disparate environments this could only be done via CTI software and the only application of any significance to emerge was that of call centers.

Readers who are interested in a very brief history of CTI, which is the backdrop of today's IP Communications stage, should read the last section of this chapter.

IP's intrinsic flexibility

The business case for IP Communications is based on the intrinsic flexibility of IP based networks. This is something that we take for granted in data communications, but the functionality it enables is revolutionary when compared to conventional telephony.

Network servers automatically assign addresses to client devices such as PCs when users log onto an IP network. These IP addresses are mapped to physical network ports; thus, the server knows where its clients are located and email will be delivered to the relevant addresses. Any port, anywhere on the local or wide area network can be used; the physical locations are only relevant for the duration of the session.

Conventional private telephony networks employ point-to-point connections over expensive leased lines. IP allows them to be replaced by virtual private network (VPN) services.

If a user logs off that particular IP address is released and can be reused. Users can move around, go to different offices in different countries and continents, and each time they log on they will get new IP addresses. Thus, the allocation of addresses is a flexible, dynamic process.

We take this for granted when using a PC, but that is not the way regular telephony works. In this case calls reach fixed, physical places and the association with a particular person is maintained in the PBX's directory, e.g. to reach John Smith dial extension 123. If our hypothetical Mr. Smith moves to another office then his entry in the directory has to be changed. Circuit-switched telephony therefore has a rigid infrastructure; it is intrinsically inflexible. IP Telephony, however, works in the same way as regular data. The IP phone is a small computer terminal having an IP address, so as soon as Mr. Smith identifies himself at the new location all his calls will be forwarded.

VPNs are also intrinsically flexible as well as being less expensive. For example, leased lines are charged around the clock, but VPN tariffs are based on usage, i.e. bandwidth is allocated on demand and billed accordingly.

IP is also allowing network operators to offer true value-added services.

So far so good, but that was just for starters. When users log onto the LAN using PCs they can use any resource on the network for which they have authorized access. That resource can be local or it may be located on the other side of the globe. The media often employs the phrase 'IP eliminates distance' to describe this facility. Once again, this is something we take for granted, but for regular telephony every location has to have a local resource, i.e. a PBX or a small 'key system' in the case of small offices.

• Issues and explanations

With IP telephony the equivalent resource is provided by one or more IP communications platforms (also computer systems) and once again they can be situated anywhere on the data network. Thus, new locations and even teleworkers become part of a worldwide real time communications network as soon as they have access to an IP network. If the company opens a new office it can come on stream in a matter of hours and even the smallest offices can have all the functionality of the headquarters.

In addition, all the communications platforms that are connected to the enterprise's network function as if they were one, huge PBX. Thus, a simple internal number scheme can be employed; there is no need to add prefixes to designate particular countries; a call to a colleague across the hall is made in the same way as one to another colleague working on another continent. But even more amazing is the fact that this functionality is intrinsic; nothing extra in the way of hardware or software has to be added.

IP Telephony applications are hosted on computer servers that are normally located (physically) at one or more large sites, e.g. a company's regional headquarters. However, all authorized users from other offices can employ them. Secure, seamless access over the Internet can also be enabled, which in turn allows road warriors to work outside the office in virtually the same way as they do when inside. The fact that the clients are fully distributed, while the servers in the client-server model are centralized, makes it easier and cheaper to manage the installation of new applications and to maintain a high level of security throughout the enterprise.

Phones as thin-client devices

IP telephony software can be employed on PCs, which enables them to be used as 'soft phones'. This is a useful function when mobile, but in the office the additional resources of the PC are employed to facilitate communications processes, e.g. set up conference calls.

In the new communications environment IP phones can be used as a regular device, i.e. pick up the handset and enter a number. However, screen sizes on some models are similar to that of PDAs and their functionality resembles that of thin-client data devices. They employ menu-driven interfaces and other PC-type features such as the ability to search the corporate directory, set up personal directories and dial by name using a softkey on the phone's display. In addition, IP phones will normally have flash memory in order to facilitate software upgrades.

Issues and explanations

This indicates that the same client-server model is employed for data and voice. The client in both cases is the IP phone. Regular enterprise servers are accessed for light data applications and a communications server is employed for telephony applications. This simple example shows how the transition to IP Communications enables enterprises to migrate towards unified Information and Communications infrastructures. It also demonstrates that voice and data can be usefully integrated within the same device. The emphasis on usefully indicates that there have been many attempts to realize integrated devices but until recently there have not been any notable successes in the marketplace.

Bluetooth is an open standard for short-range transmission of digital voice and data between mobile devices (laptops, PDAs, phones) and desktop devices.

The name Bluetooth comes from King Harald Blatan (Bluetooth) of Denmark, who lived in the 10th century.

That situation is changing. The iPAQ, for example, is a versatile PDA that employs plug-in modules to provide additional functionality. It can be used as a mobile phone and this feature is facilitated by Bluetooth technology, which allows a small wireless headset to be employed. Another module enables hot spot access to the Internet. The term hot spot refers to the implementation of wireless LAN access points in business locations such as airport lounges, hotels, conference centers and even coffee shops. In addition SIP software can be added (apologies for changing into semi-techie gear). SIP is used in IP Telephony; the phone is a thin-client data device and the communications protocol is used to set up a session (communications link) with the IP platform.

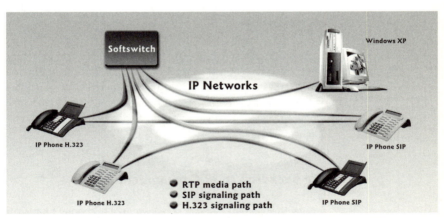

Figure 1.3.: *In IP Telephony SIP (Session Initiation Protocol) is used to set up communication sessions (communication links).*

Siemens made a demonstration of standard-based interoperability of IP phones with Microsoft PC 'soft clients' using the SIP protocol at CeBIT 2002. (See figure 1.3). SIP and therefore VoIP is supported in Windows XP. This real time communications capability is the foundation that allows people in different locations to collaborate using audio- and video-conferencing, applications sharing and online collaboration as well as email and instant messaging.

Embedded IP Telephony

Distributing the functionality of the PBX across the enterprise via servers and intelligent devices represents the all-important first step. The next involves *embedding* a set of basic services, call control, policy management and administration services directly into the enterprise's network. Embedding basic telephony functions within the network rather than supplying them in stand-alone systems represents the second step in the evolution from communication systems to communications applications and services. Enterprise servers having new, secure *real time* operating systems will be commercially available in Q1/2 2003, e.g. the new Greenwich OS component from Microsoft.

Microsoft has already signaled its real time intentions. The new server OS comes as part of the whole .NET initiative, which Microsoft positions as *"software to connect information, people, systems, and devices"*. On the client side, Windows XP has also a built-in real-time component.

Communications modules are used to enhance Microsoft's peer-to-peer core services. This software controls central tasks in the areas of call handling, security management and administration.

Communications software extensions will provide real time <u>communication modules</u> that enhance the real time functionality of new operating systems. At first sight it might seem to be a revolutionary development, and in some ways it is, but the migration from where we are today to where we want to be tomorrow can be graceful, practical, and affordable.

The backdrop to IP Communications

Getting the real time (synchronous) world of telephony to interoperate with the asynchronous world of data is not easy, but is has been clear for more than a decade that this was a very worthwhile objective. In the case of call centers integration is enabled via a CTI link, which is basically software that enables the control of telephony calls from a user desktop PC or a computer server. For incoming calls, it allows the identification of the caller to be extracted and employed by a computer server in order to access customer data. The first CTI links were very expensive and the cost could only be justified for very large call centers that served large markets, i.e. North America.

Those first links used TSAPI (Telephony Services API) and at a later date Microsoft introduced TAPI (Telephony API), which focused on the individual at the keyboard.

The next development was the development of communications servers having boards that performed the same task as a PBX. This allowed the industry to drop the I from CTI, but these computer telephony systems were not a success. The functionality did not change significantly although the use of regular servers and TAPI, which was bundled in Windows, drove prices down.

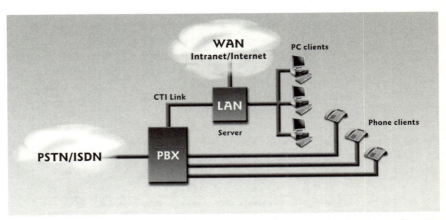

Figure 1.4.: *Regular call center solutions need computer telephony technology in order to integrate two disparate environments.*

The early objectives of computer telephony are now being realized via IP Communications and platforms that take over call control and other telephony functions from the PBX. Figure 1.5 illustrates this concept. Because voice and data now use the same communications protocol we are able to employ the productivity-enhancing applications covered in the next chapter, but we still have phones working via voice-centric platforms and data working via computer servers. Thus a purist might question the depth of the convergence, i.e. there is still a link between two different platforms, one of which, for historic reasons, is proprietary. Management and end users may not care given the functionality of the new apps.

• Issues and explanations

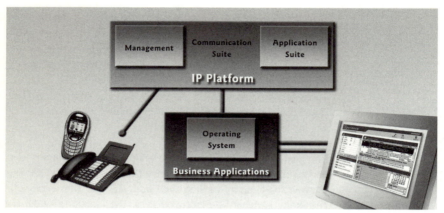

Figure 1.5.: *The end user experience is that of a unified environment, but in practice this is achieved via tight integration between two different platforms using the same communications protocol.*

However, when the servers have a real time operating system and when this is enhanced via embedded telephony functionality, then convergence could not possibly be deeper. Now there is no link because we have a one-box solution, as illustrated in figure 1.6. Note that this is a conceptual illustration; it is a single OS solution, but converged platforms and softswitch platforms are still employed.

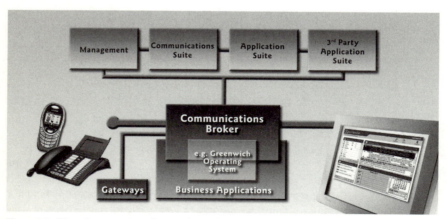

Figure 1.6.: *The end user experience does not change, but now we have one platform running both real time communications as well as data applications.*

Conclusions

The transition to an all-IP environment involves two steps. The first is the introduction of converged platforms in order to benefit from the productivity and related benefits of enhanced and new applications. Applications, which are the primary driver, are covered in the next chapter. This step will involve graceful migration from legacy platforms (PBXs) as well as the phones and telephony cabling. Migration is covered in Chapter 3.

The second step involves the introduction of new platforms that run real time communications as well as mainstream business processes. Telephony and video will then be communications services that operate in a standards-based, open-systems environment. All relevant applications will access these services in a consistent and cost-effective way.

• Issues and explanations

CHAPTER TWO
It's all about applications

This chapter shows how IP is enabling a totally new breed of synergistic, productivity-enhancing applications to be employed on phones, PCs and PDAs. It covers the shortcomings of today's point solutions and shows how communications portals are enabling anytime, anywhere access to corporate data, personal information and collaboration tools.

Applications are the key driver. As indicated earlier, this is the key benefit of IP Communications:

The speed with which new applications are created and implemented and the ease with which they are employed. New functionality can be added in virtually the same way as new plug-ins for Web browsers.

In addition IP Communications is being used to enhance existing applications such as call centers and to facilitate the implementation of others, e.g. unified messaging. Enhanced applications and brand-new developments such as managed availability divide into two main categories: those that enhance productivity and apps that serve the customer better than the competition. Most vendors offer a number of mainstream IP-enhanced applications with their solution, e.g. unified messaging (UM), unified communications (UC), and interaction centers (aka as multimedia call centers). In addition, they may carry the UC concept forward and provide multi-model (data and voice) communications portals that enable mobile access to corporate and personal data.

Published APIs and third-party development show how telephony is following the PC business model.

Vendors are also supporting mainstream APIs in order to facilitate the development of applications by third parties. Applications communicate with a computer's operating system via APIs and

• It's all about applications

programmers write to the interface; this removes the need to know anything about platform hardware or the network to which it is connected. This means that there will be no shortage of innovative communications applications. APIs are also used to 'telephony enable' business processes such as CRM, ERP, Supply Chain Management and E-commerce.

As we shall see in this chapter, IP-enabled applications employ the familiar browser interface, so usage is intuitive. This is an important, generic benefit since applications that are easy to use get used. These Web-based apps will also make increasing use of Web services. This is a relatively recent concept and it is backed by all the major IT players, e.g. IBM, Microsoft, Oracle and Sun. There are competing technologies and standards as well as broad agreements on the future direction.

Applets that build on each other to form value-added chains can also be customized.

The basic idea is to create application modules (aka applets) that interoperate with each other and which can be used to build bigger applications. For example, one module might provide an authentication function; others could perform currency conversions and language translations. One Web service that many readers may have used is the form that requests personal information. Once completed the Web browser can reuse this auto-form service to facilitate access to other sites.

The ability to communications enable business processes will not only improve operational efficiency, but it will also lead to the development of leaner, meaner ways of working.

These are data-centric examples, but a similar development effort will enable real time applets to be brought into various communications tasks and to be integrated with data applets. For example, a customer may complain about late delivery to the call center; the agent generates a trouble ticket and enters the relevant details; the data is automatically forwarded to the ERP system, which generates a response; this is forwarded to the relevant salesperson who then calls the customer. The process is quick and efficient and customers do not need to keep on repeating the same information, e.g. one time to the call center agent and then again to the salesperson.

Analysts are drawing parallels between the declining use of mainframe applications and those of packed applications; the latter started around 1998. The development of component applications and Web services started at the same time and usage looks set to overtake conventional packaged applications in 2005/6. By that time the technology will have advanced to the point where end users are able to create their own applications easily and quickly. No programming skills will be required.

The speed with which applications are created currently comes via standards and published APIs. This is not a brand-new telephony development, but the transition to IP telephony means that developers are able to use the same programming languages for voice as they did for data. And the APIs, which IP platform vendors define, remove the need to understand the ins and outs of real-time communications. This simple model illustrates that concept.

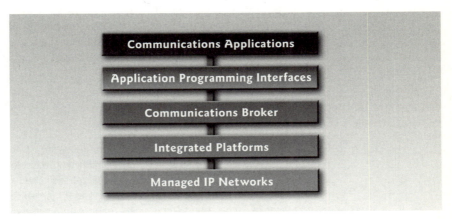

IP telephony is an evolutionary development that has revolutionary implications. Intuitive usage of real time applications ensures rapid acceptance of the new functionality, which in turn leads to enhanced productivity and a fast return on investment.

Adding new functionality in virtually the same way as new plug-ins for Web browsers is a revolutionary concept from a telecommunications perspective, but it is relatively easy to bring real-time communications into Web environments via the support for other Internet standards. Equally important is the fact that usage of all new applications is intuitive since the familiar browser interface is used. The section on Communications Portals illustrates this important benefit.

It is clear that there will be no shortage of applications. The programming community that helped create the PC market has set its $ sights on IP Communications. The same standards and languages are employed and APIs remove the need to know anything about the intricacies of real-time communications, the platforms and the networks.

• It's all about applications

Boosting productivity and providing better services to the market are generic benefits that no company can ignore. However, decision makers within companies have to balance the business and financial returns against the cost of implementing new systems and amortizing earlier investments in telephony systems. In the current economic climate the scales would appear to come down on the financial side, i.e. the benefits are hard to ignore but the cost is too high. That would be true if it was necessary to replace perfectly good telephony systems with IP platforms, but this is not the case. The concept may be revolutionary but implementation can be evolutionary. Before considering IP-enabled applications this chapter will therefore outline a low-entry point strategy that demonstrates how the benefits of this important development can be evaluated at a pilot site, e.g. a department or remote office. Chapter 3 will illustrate various practical migration strategies that can be adopted after the pilot.

Test drive the benefits

In most enterprises the information and communications infrastructure comprises two separate networks employing different technologies and communications protocols. There is the telephone network, which is based on circuit-switched technology and PBXs, which are proprietary systems. And there is a data (information) network, which employs packet switching and computer servers, which are open systems.

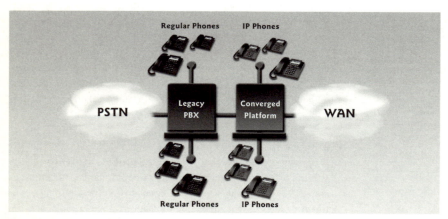

Figure 2.1.: *Converged platforms enable interworking with legacy PBXs. This allows IP Communications to be introduced and evaluated at departmental level or in one or more remote locations.*

It's all about applications •

Converged platforms protect investments in legacy phones and cabling as well as PBXs. This is an important feature since the new functionality is normally not required by all employees.

Figure 2.1 shows how an organization might elect to connect a so-called IP Converged platform to a PBX in order to allow IP Communications to be introduced at various departmental levels. The term indicates that hybrid approach, i.e. the use of circuit and packet switching in the same system. One side connects to the PSTN and the other to the WAN. Legacy phones remain in place or they can be connected to the new platform via the circuit switched interface. IP Phones connect to the packet switching interface. This allows new IP devices to be employed in one or more departments, those that would benefit most from the new functionality. Thus, converged platforms are an ideal way to trial the concept and evaluate the benefits.

Seamless and synergistic

There is analogy to the stand-alone applications created for the DOS environment and the synergy of Microsoft Office in the Windows environment.

It is relatively complex and therefore expensive to develop computer telephony applications when voice and data occupy disparate domains. This is why few desktops have unified messaging (UM), i.e. a single inbox for email, facsimile and voicemail. UM is useful, but it does not represent a groundbreaking communications application. Implementing UM will make an incremental reduction in transaction costs, which is the primary goal of IP Communications, but a holistic approach is required. First-generation applications could only chip away at the problem via a series of point solutions; convergence enables not only the creation of any application that makes sense, but also seamless, synergistic interoperation between applications. And in future we can anticipate the development of application components that are shared, thereby eliminating the need to reinvent various parts of the communication wheel.

First generation computer telephony applications such as a virtual personal assistant would try to find the called party but the functionality was very limited.

In order to see how synergy and seamless interworking are being applied to real-time communications we are going to revisit the problem of telephone tag. Recall the John-Julie scenario. John calls Julie and gets her voicemail. He leaves a 'please call me back' message. Julie calls back and gets John's voice mail. She tells him that 'I called you back but you were busy'. If John and Julie are busy people getting in touch may take some time, and if the reason for calling is urgent the delay could be serious. If it is urgent then John may ring Julie's mobile number and there's a good chance that he'll get voicemail again, but this time on a second system and so it goes on. Eventually Julie will call back, after listening to different voicemails on different systems and maybe reading emails and instant messages as well.

• It's all about applications

The key parameter that allows this communications circle to be broken is the presence of the called party on the network. Instant messaging (IM) is a simple and relatively new application for the business environment. Users establish a list of people with whom they want to communicate (buddies) and as shown in figure 2.2, their presence on the corporate network is flagged as soon as they logon. Thus, John can see if Julie is on-line and if she is, they can send text messages back and forth.

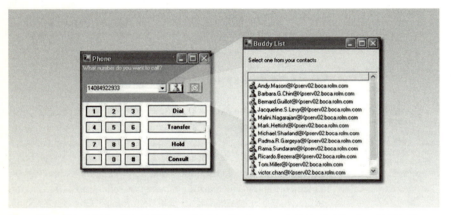

Figure 2.2.: *The red IM flag shows colleagues who are not on-line; green indicates that they have logged onto the network. This baseline function can be extended to indicate availability to receive telephone calls.*

The combination of voice-data presence solves the problem of telephone tag at a stroke. John does not waste time calling Julie if she is talking; he waits until she is free; nor does he waste time by trying the mobile because he knows that Julie is logged on, i.e. she is on the wireline network.

In IP Communications the phone and the PC interoperate. An IP phone is a thin-client data device and the PC can be a softphone. Thus, data-side presence can be linked to voice-side presence. If Julie is logged on John can see if Julie is talking or if her phone is not in use. The functionality will normally be part of a unified messaging inbox, as shown in figure 2.3. Note that presence for both IM and voice are flagged.

Presence is a very useful application that boosts productivity and reduces transaction costs, but it is just the tip of the communications and collaboration iceberg. Collaboration sessions can be established using the various 'buddies' and messages can also be filtered so that they appear in the relevant collaboration folder. Personal and group agendas can also be displayed. In addition, the system will normally make the decision as to which media type to use; this is based on the called party's preference. However, the calling party can bypass this automated feature, select a particular media type and the system will then decide on the best type of device for that media type. For

It's all about applications •

Figure 2.3.: *Microsoft's IM application is known as Windows Messenger and it is bundled with Windows XP, which is a real time operating system. This facilitates the integration of data and telephony presence.*

example, the called party may prefer IM but the caller selects email; the system might send this to a PDA but not a phone.

Without presence a two-party communication can involve multiple voicemails on different systems and other message types being sent to different devices. Too much time is lost and both parties get stressed and frustrated. Setting up a conference call in order to address a serious issue becomes a nightmare and decisions might be taken without all relevant parties being involved. This is particularly true when parties are mobile. The IM-phone link allows small group sessions to be set up manually (you see who is free and click to call) or it can be automated. The latter is ideal for larger conference calls. An IM is sent to the relevant parties informing them of the need to collaborate and the system sets up the conference call when all parties are free. Mobile presence can also be detected, but in this case a business agreement is needed with the mobile network operator. This subject is covered later in the section on the mobile office.

Managed availability

Technology can be a double-edged sword: witness the explosive growth in emails. Research from IDC predicts a rise from the current figure of 31 billion/day to 60 billion/day by 2006. One third of those figures is spam. If the world knows your email address then you are going to get lots of emails and one clearly does not want the same thing to apply to telephony, particularly since this is an

• It's all about applications

intrusive medium. Thus, while it is a good thing for colleagues to know if you are present and if you are free (available) to talk, the ability to manage one's availability and thereby enable privacy for the wider world is better.

The following five steps illustrate how vendors are addressing this issue.

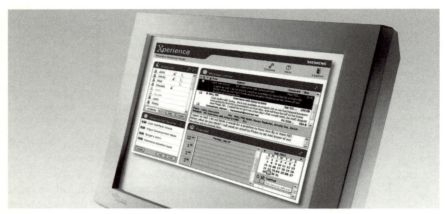

Step 1: *users create a contact list on their PC and give specific instructions as to the options that should be offered to these callers, e.g. my partner, my boss can reach me at all times. Users only give out a single, virtual number. The system presents the relevant options to the caller when this number is called. Thus, a single communications portal enables access to phones, voicemail, pager, IM and basic email. This makes it much easier for callers on the contact list and gives users more control over disruptive interruptions. It also minimizes having the same message left on different services.*

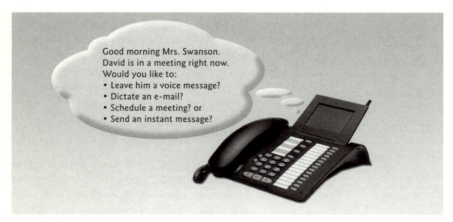

Step 2: *for Kim Swanson the options are: leave a message, schedule a meeting, dictate an email or send an instant message. This user (David) has not authorized mobile/cellular calls from Kim, nor has this number been given out. Access to confidential information is secured using voiceprint authentication.*

It's all about applications •

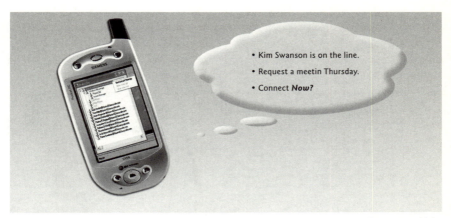

Step 3: *HiPath informs the called party that Kim is on the line by sending an instant message to his voice-enabled PDA. David can then take Kim out of this automated transaction and talk to her using his device of choice. Natural language interfaces enable a wide range of options to be employed even on very basic devices. In addition, device mediation is used to adapt the form, length and features of the communiqué to match the preferred device. In this case the device is a PDA and IM is employed.*

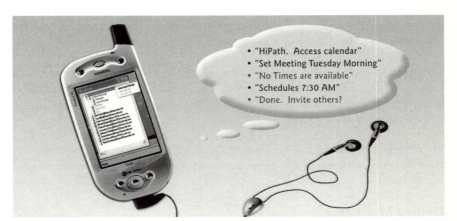

Step 4: *David and Kim decide to meet on Tuesday, not Thursday. David simply tells the system to access his calendar and then schedules the meeting using spoken commands. This indicates how IP-enabled voice becomes an integral part of the information infrastructure. David could also tap a time slot on his PDA's calendar.*
Once scheduled, the solution could reserve a meeting room or accommodate other user preferences. Other parties can also be invited to the meeting. The groupware calendar functions create an invitation and user then dictates the subject and message.

• It's all about applications

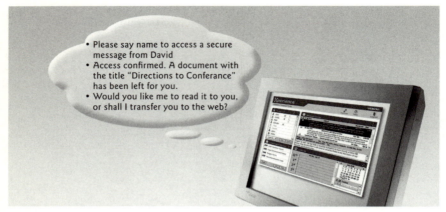

Step 5: *Users can leave different information for different callers, by recording the message in the voicemail system or by placing it on a Web page. An all-IP information and communications environment means that devices can be transferred from the voice system directly to a Web page in order to view or download additional information.*

In addition, presence can be linked to agendas. The system would typically make the wireline phone the primary device when in the office and the cellular phone would be the primary device when on the move. Only important calls would be put through when in the office and none at all when unavailable, e.g. on a plane.

The buddy list concept can be applied to agendas, thereby allowing members of a team to look into each other's availability in order to set up meetings without going through a round of telephony calls. The system can also inform participants of any external addition to their agenda by e-mail or SMS.

When customizable, personal portals are combined with managed presence the result is a very powerful communications tool that minimizes wasted time and increases productivity.

Unified Messaging

Unified Messaging did not reach many corporate desktops despite its ability to increase employee productivity significantly. This came from the fact that voice and data occupied disparate environments, which meant that the cost of integration and network management overshadowed the benefits. A converged network, however, provides the necessary platform for this application.

It's all about applications •

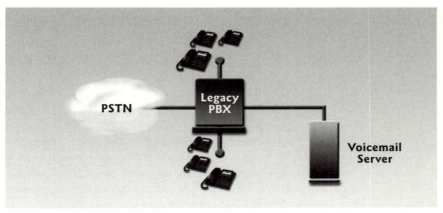

Figure 2.4.: *Legacy voicemail is based on proprietary servers attached to PBXs, which are proprietary switching systems.*

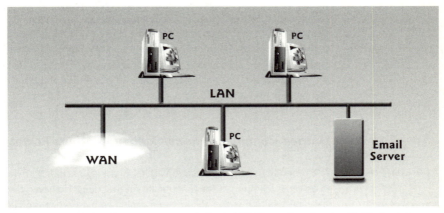

Figure 2.5.: *Email is based on open servers attached to the LAN. Thus, voicemail and email sit in disparate environments, thereby making integration a costly exercise.*

Voice mail belongs to the circuit-switched domain of figure 2.4. For historic reasons this application normally ran on a proprietary computer platform attached to the PBX. E-mail would be one of the applications running on the LAN-attached communications server, as shown in figure 2.5. Clever engineering can unify both message types at the client level but this is an integration solution, not a unified solution. Both directories are managed separately.

In a converged environment voice mail runs on the same platform as email, so the solution is integrated at the source and manage-

• It's all about applications

ment costs are much lower. This means that unified messaging is an automatic by-product of convergence.

The ability to view and process all message types in a single inbox allows voicemail to be selected in the same way as e-mail, i.e. users are no longer forced to listen to these messages sequentially. This indicates that the increase in productivity comes via time saved, which is considerable. A study published in the Wall Street Journal found that the average employee sends and receives more than 200 messages per day; another study from Comgroup found that office workers experienced a 53% time-saving when using UM and the figure was 70% for mobile users. UM also allows faxes and voicemails to be forwarded and archived in the same way as emails.

UM is a point solution; messages are unified but there is no additional functionality. UM's effectiveness can be extended using text-to-voice technology, which enables Unified Communications (covered in the next section), but it can also be seen as a workaround. More useful is the ability to have a multi-modal (text and telephony) interface that can be used by the new multi-modal devices, i.e. PDAs that are voice enabled. Why listen to emails over the phone when they can be seen on screen?.

Unified Communications/Communications Portal

A **communications portal** is a superior solution to UM/UC. It has a multi-modal interface, making it ideal for the new generation of PDAs. Moreover, mobile employees only have to logon once to access everything they need, i.e. corporate and personal data in addition to messages.

The term Unified Communications (UC) is widely used, but there is no clear definition of the functionality it describes. However, the baseline function is the ability to process messages while mobile, e.g. listen to emails from a cellular/mobile phone and give voice command such as Next, Delete and Reply. It can be provided by regular computer telephony technology, but the concept is being carried forward using IP Communications and for this reason terms such as Communications Portals are now employed.

As illustrated in figure 2.6, an enterprise class communications portal provides a common point of access to all authorized communications services and applications that the user requires. Functionality includes device mediation, media translation and access via a single logon.

Device mediation is used to provide the appropriate communications features to the user's device, i.e. the system recognizes the resources such as screen size. Media translation includes text to speech to

It's all about applications •

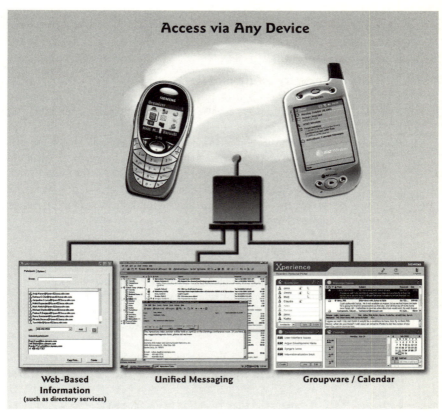

Figure 2.6. Communications portals enable anytime, anywhere access to corporate data, personal information and collaborative tools.

speech to text. The single logon enables access to all network-based functions, basic telephony features, one number office/cellular access, and enterprise applications that employ embedded communications functions.

Individuals and enterprises can create simple or complex voice portal applications using standard Web authoring tools and templates for regular call processing applications. Portals can also be customized. Thus, everybody in the organization can have fast, easy access to the information and services they need. A salesman, for example, can go directly to the relevant part of a database using a cellular phone and listen to price and delivery information. A salesperson can listen to his/her new messages when on the move. This can be done several times a day in order to make sure that the really important messages are heard in time.

Security while mobile

A fob was originally a short strap or chain. It is now used to describe a small data device that is easy to carry around and would typically be attached to a key ring.

Security is always a valid concern, particularly when public air interfaces are being used, i.e. wireless hot spots or cellular networks. End-to-end security solutions are available, but those that are based on client-server software cannot be employed when the client device is a regular cellular/mobile phone. In this case a key fob employing token-based authentication/encryption is highly secure as well as convenient it can also be employed when a voice-centric device is used.

The fob displays a randomly generated access code that changes every 60 seconds. The user logs in by entering a secret personal identification number (PIN) followed by the current code displayed on the display. The logon process is therefore both simple and totally secure. Nothing resides on the client device so secure access is enabled from third-party devices such as those employed in Internet cafes.

Call centers become customer interaction centers

Although early promises were not realized, CRM remains a mission-critical application since it focuses on customer retention and loyalty.

Call centers and their evolution of multimedia contact centers (aka interaction centers) represent the application that is used to gain and maintain a company's sales and marketing edge. In addition, interaction centers leverage investments made in CRM systems.

Call centers take on an entirely new meaning when IP Communications enters the picture. Estimates vary, but there are between one to two million agents working in a centralized facility, i.e. a physical center. However, anybody who is on the IP LAN or WAN can be an agent; the location is irrelevant so there is no need for a physical center. Calls can therefore be handled around the world and around the clock. Agents can be added or removed in seconds. Skills-based routing also becomes much easier. If the relevant expert has logged onto the network then his/her location is known immediately. Calls can even be forwarded to mobile phones. In addition, it is easy to add teleworkers at peak periods, e.g. in the summer months for travel agents, at the end of the year for a mail-order company. All

It's all about applications •

that's needed is a multimedia PC or IP phone and broadband, secure access to the corporate network.

The new functionality (and there's more, much more) comes from IP's intrinsic flexibility and the use of a single network. This point has been made before and it won't be made again, but since this is the last time let's underline its significance. A converged network virtualizes a company's resources, both human and electronic. Call center functionality, for example, can be distributed and the center itself scaled down to individual sales agents. The physical locations of all communications applications and the people that employ them are not important and therefore the 'center' in call center' is becoming less relevant.

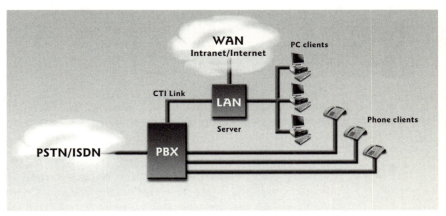

Figure 2.7.: *Regular call center solutions need computer telephony technology in order to integrate two disparate environments: the PSTN and that of corporate networks. The degree of integration, however, is minimal, e.g. when calls are transferred to another agent the relevant customer file is not forwarded at the same time.*

This scenario is basically the same as that of unified messaging. The application relies on computer telephony glue in order to join up two disparate environments: those of voice and data. However, in this case the benefits of call centers exceed the cost of integration and network management.

Figure 2.7 is that of a regular call center. Calls come in from the PSTN and the PBX directs them to an agent. There is a CTI (computer telephony integration) link between the PBX and the server. This is used to tell the computer side (e.g. the CRM system) the ID of the caller so that the relevant record can be retrieved and 'popped up' on the PC screen of the relevant agent. Clever and therefore expensive engineering is needed to make this work. The call center has to 'speak' to computer databases and make routing decisions; this is a complex process and scaling is far from easy. This indicates that it is hard to maintain interaction with customers when the customer data and the requisite staff are located in different parts of the enterprise.

• It's all about applications

Put the whole thing together on a converged infrastructure, as illustrated in figure 2.8, and everything changes. The difficult integration process is eliminated since voice and data are integrated at the network level. This enables database records to travel with transferred calls.

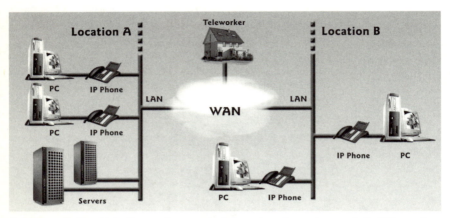

Figure 2.8.: *An IP-enabled call center allows agents to be located anywhere on the network. The IP Communications and Application Servers are normally hosted in the corporate data center. Teleworkers have the same functionality as their colleagues and can offer the same level of service to callers.*

Location independence is clearly a key benefit. A center can be any size and be physically connected to any part of the network, but the ability to support multiple contact channels is becoming increasingly important, hence the change of name to Customer Interaction Center. Customers and prospects now want to communicate via Web collaboration, text chat, email and even video communications. Plain vanilla telephony does not cut it anymore, although the phone is the primary communications medium and will remain so for many if not most sites.

As indicated earlier, a converged network virtualizes human as well as electronic resources. This allows an organization to maintain a larger pool of skilled agents, for example, technical specialists can become temporary agents when important customers or prospects need answers to tricky questions. Companies who are able to interact in this way are clearly much more likely to retain existing customers and convert enquiries into sales. Another key feature is the ability to analyze the contents of emails, prior to routing, to see if it matches Frequently Asked Questions. This increases the productivity of agents, as does the addition of an email contact channel. Agents can juggle 3 to 4 emails simultaneously but can only handle one phone call

It's all about applications

at a time. The use of email also allows the number of phone lines to be reduced. This indicates that the first word in the term 'call center' is less relevant.

The automated distribution process, which is common for phone calls, is also available for voice mail, fax messages, email and Web forms. This ensures the most efficient use of agents and counteracts the problem of leaving email unchecked and processing them later. All messages, including voice mail in the form of wave files, exist as data packets, so they can be processed uniformly and sent via email or answered with a call. It is also possible to save a call as voice mail when the call center is overloaded and to forward it.

A single customer view and ubiquitous CRM

Frost & Sullivan expect the European revenues of these Web-based call centers to rise from US$57 million in 2000 to roughly US$317 million by 2002.

Research conducted by analysts at PricewaterhouseCoopers shows that while only 11% of all European call centers were Web-enabled in 1999, this figure should increase to 46% by 2003.

These figures equate to increased use of email, however, tests carried out by Incovis found that two thirds of email orders or inquiries receive no response.

The evolution of call centers in multimedia, interactive contact centers is a very positive development, as is the ability to distribute agents around the network. However, it does not address fundamental issues such as the fact that CRM projects have tended to focus on immediate, specific operational goals; ideally this application should be part of a broader, customer management framework. This is the main reason why first call or first contact resolution of customer issues remains an elusive goal for many companies despite the massive investments in new systems that have been made in recent years.

We operate in a service economy, but according to research conducted by Purdue University 68% of customer defections are related to service issues; only 16% relate to products and 9% to price. The key dissatisfaction issue is the inability to access the right person and obtain the right information! Muddling through the organization, finding the right person to address the issue and executing follow-up calls is expensive, inconvenient and unreliable — for both the company and its customers. Moreover, customer expectations are rising and the speed of the Internet has resulted in the need for immediate responses to more questions and for more self-service options.

These somewhat alarming statistics indicate that there is a need to rethink the contact center model — to create true holistic solutions. Customers evaluate the service they received based on their total experience and companies are realizing that processes and job roles that span large parts of the organization either impact on or support the customer in some way. However, the largest percentage

• It's all about applications

Jupiter Research found that only 52% received a reply within 24 hours and 32% took three days or longer. Yet very convenient tools exist to handle the various steps involved in processing email. messages are available.

of knowledge, experience and problem solving is not found within the average call center and most so-called solutions do not enable additional customer interactions. Many agents are not allowed to transfer calls and would not know whom to contact if they were. This indicates that a truly consumer-centric organization needs to expand beyond the confines of the center and enable interaction between 'high-value' customers and its experts/specialists. In addition, there is a clear need to provide a single view of the customer across the organization's multiple touch points.

It is ironic that while the industry has recognized these needs, the technology introduced in recent years actually reduces contact between customers and the company's employees. Automated IVR systems, for example, are not user friendly. At the same time many if not most agents are the least skilled and least experienced employees; they are also poorly paid and the average stay is between one and two years. The cost of running call centers is obviously important, but when performance and service gaps lead to a failure to close a sale then the center starts to become a liability.

The way out of this spiral is to identify the relevant skills of the company's knowledge workers and specialists and to match them with the incoming customer's needs, i.e. to enable immediate contact with the right person so that the right information is obtained. Looking ahead, it is essential that every employee that might impact customer service and influence relationships must have access to that

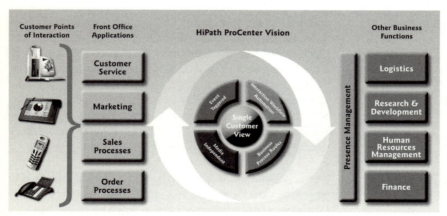

Figure 2.9.: *The proposed holistic solution creates a single, enterprise-wide view of all relevant customer information, which it stores and processes through ubiquitous CRM applications. In this way organizations will have a much better opportunity to better service and retain customers, which is the foundation for long-term success and profitability.*

unified customer via a common sets of tools that have been deployed throughout the organization. This ubiquitous CRM capability will ultimately become as widespread as word processing for spreadsheet application software on the desktops of managers and knowledge workers and also be extended to mobile environments.

This vision, which goes beyond the call and interaction center concept, is visualized in figure 2.9. This show that all customer-facing processes must be extended to allow broader access to the organization; they should also link with suppliers, branch offices and the relevant business partners. The illustration also indicates that the current focus on the addition of multimedia channels does not address the core issues; instead it bolts new functionality onto a flawed architecture. The proposed holistic solution creates a single, enterprise-wide view of customer-related information and processes through ubiquitous CRM applications.

Teleworking/Telecommuting

IP Communications meshes perfectly with the teleworking/ telecommuting trend and the concept of location-independent business models, e.g. virtual offices. The Gartner Group predicts that there will be almost 150 million telecommuters by 2003 and the Yankee Group estimates that there are around 1.6 million branch offices in the Fortune 500 companies.

Teleworking and telecommuting are two work practices that are good for enterprises and good for the environment. Cut down commuting times and you can boost productivity, minimize stress at the same time, and help retain key employees. An all-round win:win scenario, but working at home is more complicated than working in the office, mainly because telephony is based on location-centric systems — PBXs. Intranets have facilitated access to computing resources that might be located in another country or even another continent, and VPNs enable secure access from remote sites, but these decentralized developments focused on data-only applications.

The heart of the problem lies with telephony's intrinsic rigidity, e.g. separate dial-ins are needed to access voice mail and the corporate network. ISDN lines were promoted as being a teleworking solution but the concept was not widely adopted outside central Europe, one reason being high communications costs. IP Communications, however, enables both voice and data applications to be decentralized and the same information and communications network is employed for remote access. In a converged environment all a teleworker needs is a multimedia PC, a router, and on-line access to the Internet. All the communications functionality that they employ in the office is then provided at home or in a small office. It really is that easy and that simple.

• It's all about applications

Video meetings and teleconferencing

In the last decade the enterprise telephony network has continued to evolve, enabling voice communications to continue to increase its efficiency, functionality, and simplicity as it migrates to an IP-based paradigm. Now we are seeing the same trend in video communications. Videoconferencing technology has migrated from legacy ISDN (Integrated Services Digital Network) to a fully converged IP network; enterprises are able to not only reduce their network access costs by eliminating costly ISDN connections but also deliver video communication and video collaboration tools to enterprise desktops.

ISDN is a well-established digital telecommunications standard. It enables data to be transported at rates of between 128 kbps and 2 Mbps, which is low by today's standards. ISDN is based on circuit-switched technology and is expensive compared to packet-switched services.

Video communication, with voice and data, may be used for multiple applications using either meeting rooms that have dedicated equipment or an end-user desktop environment. For example:

- Conferences; as a replacement to face-to-face meeting

- Collaboration; desktop-based data collaboration and converged communications among two or more users

- Distance learning; enables the training of multiple people in multiple locations

- Telemedicine; enables consultation, second opinion and remote healthcare.

- Finance; investor relations, video teller

- Engineering; design teams.

The cost of video conferencing comes down significantly when an IP service replaces ISDN lines and once again we see the intrinsic flexibility of IP Communications. Implementing Video over IP is a logical next step for many companies. It leverages the same LAN/WAN infrastructure, thereby improving the ROI, and for desktop meetings the systems upgrade cost is minimal.

The business case for moving onwards and upwards, from voice over IP to video over IP, is clear. This is a relatively new medium, but at the same time it is a very natural way to communicate and one can therefore anticipate fast acceptance by end users and a further reduction in transaction costs via the increase in productivity.

When video is available at all relevant desktops it will be employed, particularly by users who are collaborating on one or more projects. And we can expect to see a number of software enhancements to be developed and marketed in the near term. For example, systems will detect who is talking and display the relevant head and shoulders shot in the desktop window. This facility is employed in professional videoconferencing systems.

Conclusions

Intel's Andy Grove once said, *"If it can be done it will be done."* One can paraphrase that remark and say, "If there's a market for a real time communications application it will be developed". Telephony and video are set to go down the same innovation path as the PC on both hard- and software fronts. The proprietary world of PBXs is transitioning to open platforms, i.e. real time operating systems running on enterprise servers. IP and other important standards such as Parlay are already enabling holistic solutions that cut right through traditional communications barriers.

It is hard to exaggerate the impact on business; it really will be seismic. For years the industry over-hyped its claims; now it is over-delivering, as evidenced by the amazing functionality of managed presence and communications portals.

Q.E.D.

CHAPTER THREE
Migration: the #1 issue

This chapter examines the only significant issue: how to realize the productivity and other benefits of IP Communications and at the same time protect the legacy investment in regular telephony systems, phones and cabling. In other words, how to minimize the opex yet still drive transaction costs way down. Capex cost comparisons are also included.

In a green field site location IP Communications would normally be implemented immediately and an ROI of three to six months would be typical. However, since telephony is a necessary condition of conducting business and there is no legacy investment to be protected in new offices this calculation is somewhat meaningless. Nobody ever tried to work out ROIs for traditional PBX, but the respective costs of installing these systems and maintaining them versus a Centrex service was considered in the past. Centrex, which is less well known in Europe than N. America, is a service provided by the local telephone company.

In this case the switching is done in the network. In some cases switching is performed on site; but calls are always controlled from the network. Similar IP Centrex services are available and calls are controlled by an IP server hosted in the network. IP Centrex is a viable option, particularly for small- and medium-sized businesses; however, given the current climate, one obvious consideration is the ability of the service provider to stay in business. At the end of the day it comes down to the respective merits of owning something (platforms and phones) or leasing something (a service).

• Migration: the #1 issue

Some vendors of IP platforms offer managed network services. In this case the vendor installs and maintains the infrastructure and performance is monitored against service level agreements.

In the past one could rely on the service provider (the former PTT) to survive, but handing over something as critical as communications to a third-party is something many companies are loath to do. On the other hand technical resources are required to manage the new converged networks and many companies may come up short in that department. Managed services are an attractive alternative. The hardware is leased, so there is no capex, and it sits on the company's network, i.e. everything is on site. Costs and other key areas such as service level agreements are made and if the service provider fails to reach the agreed performance level there is a clause that enables the company to look around for an alternative provider. The key difference is that the hardware stays on the company's premises and there is no service disruption.

The market has invested around $250 billion in circuit-switched hardware; that is an estimate of the world's installed base of PBXs and this figure clearly indicates that migrating to the new packet-switched platforms is a process that needs to be considered very carefully.

Companies who have been conducting business for some time will have made significant investments in their telephony systems — PBXs, phones and cabling. Management should therefore balance the need to protect their investment while at the same time recognizing that IP Communications is a development that they cannot afford to ignore. Thus, this is the big question: How to get from here to there in the most cost-effective way?

If you are adding a new location to your corporate network, i.e. a green field site, this is a great way to evaluate the benefits of IP Communications, but in other situations the migration process is more complex and no two situations are the same so this book can only provide generic advice.

IP-enable the PBXs

Enterprises have traditionally used expensive leased lines to create private telephony networks. As illustrated in figure 3.1, each PBX pair requires its own line so large networks have many dedicated point-to-point links. And as well as being expensive, particularly when national borders are crossed, the architecture of private networks is intrinsically inflexible: for example, every site has to be managed locally and every new site requires its own switching facility, even if the number of users is a mere handful. Networking was therefore simple, but it was not efficient. Companies had to have sufficient capacity to handle traffic peaks, but outside regular office hours this precious resource was hardly employed.

Migration: the #1 issue •

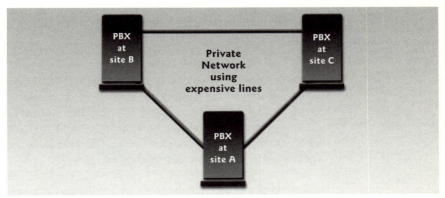

Figure 3.1.: *Enterprises have traditionally used expensive leased lines to create private telephony networks. The architecture is inflexible; new lines are needed for every new site and implementing a global network is problematic.*

When the same vendor supplies the PBXs a super-set of an industry-standard networking protocol can be used and this enables a network of PBXs to be configured and used as if it were one large switch. A private numbering scheme can be employed, which eliminates the need to add dialing prefixes to international calls and calls can be transferred across the network in the same way as local calls.

In figure 3.2 we see the same three sites connected with a wide area network. In this case the network is semi-public, i.e. many companies share the physical resource of the service provider, but functionally it is both secure and private. Thus, each company has its own virtual private network.

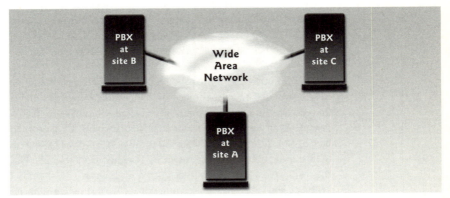

Figure 3.2.: *Adding VoIP gateways allows PBXs to be networked over a packet-switched wide area network. The operating cost of this service is much lower; transparent dialing and other features are retained.*

• Migration: the #1 issue

Calls between sites are said to be 'on net'. Calls that break out to the public network are said to be 'off net'. The VPN is also used for off net calls, i.e. the PSTN is bypassed until the call reaches the nearest corporate site. A local or national charge is then incurred.

Modern PBXs can be 'IP-enabled' by adding a VoIP gateway. The basic idea is very simple: telephony signals are digitized and converted into the packet format employed for IP transmissions. When a call from site A arrives at site B the equivalent gateway converts the VoIP traffic back into a circuit-switched format. The key benefit is a much lower communications bill. VoIP allows companies to consolidate their voice and data circuits and eliminates the need to interconnect PBXs using expensive leased lines. In Europe an E1 line supports 30 users but an IP-based network can accommodate the same number for around one tenth of the cost.

This is a logical and necessary first step and the decision to take it is rendered painless by the significant reduction in the size of the monthly telephony bill. The only issue is the need for the service to be engineered to handle the additional traffic and for quality of service mechanisms that give priority to voice traffic to be in place.

Replacing fixed capacity leased lines with VoIP trunks eliminates the need to engineer and pay for the maximum capacity needed in the typical office day. Traffic will typically peak for a few hours but with a leased line the company pays for 24-hour usage. VoIP trunks can be engineered to provide bandwidth on demand, i.e. the company only pays for what it uses.

Extending the reach

In addition to slashing the phone bill, VoIP gateways allow companies to combine the reliability and feature set of their telephony systems with the flexibility of IP technology. They do not, however, enable IP-enhanced applications to be deployed and used. That comes later in this hypothetical (but practical) migration strategy.

The PC revolution that started about 20 years ago allowed computing to be distributed down to the level of an individual employee working from home. As a result, the majority of large enterprises are highly decentralized, i.e. they have a lot of small branch offices in order to be close to the customer. These sites are normally well served on the data side but the reverse is true for telephony. Instead of a PBX they will have a key system that does not network with the other switches and which has limited functionality. Thus, while PBXs are doing an excellent job for the main sites, other equally important parts of the organization are disadvantaged. However, the remote sites will normally have a wideband link (e.g. DSL) to the VPN and this facility can be used to transport voice. One would therefore expect to see solutions that enable PBX features and functionality to be extended out to those remote locations using the same data link.

In future network operators will provide a hosted gateway service. IP platforms will connect to the network via so-called IP pipes.

The PBX vendor will normally provide this facility, which will be incorporated in the company's VoIP gateway. Solutions are also available from third parties. In both cases voice packets and PBX applications are transported to remote clients over a managed IP network. This gives branch offices the appearance of being located at a central facility such as the headquarters.

Adding the new apps

Lower operating expenses and extending the reach is good, but IP-enabled applications are better and the all-important second step can only start when there is voice-data convergence on the other side of the PBXs, i.e. on the LAN. Unless there are valid reasons to simply replace the PBXs, which is seldom the case, the convergence strategy will need to protect legacy investments while at the same time enabling a smooth transition to IP Communications.

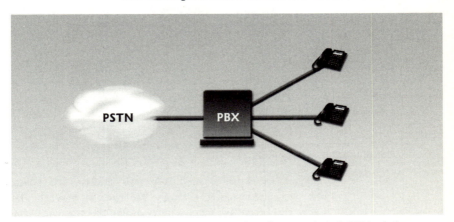

Figure 3.3.: Circuit-switched telephony. In this architecture the intelligence resides in the PBX (a telephony mainframe) that serves locally attached phones (dumb terminals).

We are talking about bringing two disparate environments together and getting them to interoperate, so let us start by reviewing the basics of those two separate networks. In figure 3.3 we see the regular telephone network, which is based on circuit-switched tech-

• Migration: the #1 issue

nology and PBXs, which are proprietary systems. Phones connect to PBXs in a star configuration, so the investment in cabling is not inconsiderable.

Figure 3.4 shows a data (information) network, which employs packet switching and computer servers, which are open systems. Most enterprises employ LAN switches in order to give each workstation a dedicated resource, e.g. 10 PCs each get their own 10 Mbps of bandwidth from the main 100 Mbps connection. This is known as a switched LAN configuration and it must be employed before IP Communications is implemented. The original LAN architecture involved resource sharing, which was fine for 'bursty' data traffic, i.e. one workstation would grab the resource when the others were idle and use it for the required duration. It is clear that this would not work for voice traffic; one conversation could not be allowed to block the others.

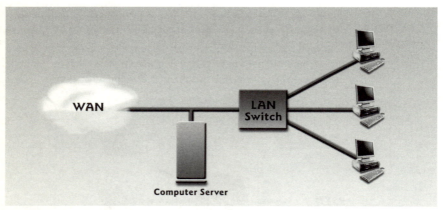

Figure 3.4.: *Data processing and communications employs the client-server architecture. The services provided by computer servers can be employed by any authorized user on the LAN and WAN. The local and remote devices are intelligent devices, e.g. PCs.*

Computer servers that live on the LAN host databases and applications. They also enable access to the WAN and the Internet. The PCs are also known as clients, which explains why the term client-server is employed.

Converged platforms

Voice-data convergence is enabled by IP communications platforms. These systems live on the LAN and use this physical medium to

Migration: the #1 issue •

transport voice traffic. These platforms can either be native IP systems, i.e. they only handle IP traffic, or they can be converged platforms. The latter are a relatively new development. They combine circuit and packet switching in the same system, i.e. one half functions as a regular PBX and the other as an IP PBX. Thus, regular phones connect to the circuit-switched interface as per figure 3.3, while the IP phones connect to the packet-switched interface (via the LAN switch) as shown in figure 3.5. Note that this does not introduce any interoperability issues; there is seamless 'mix and match' between the different client devices.

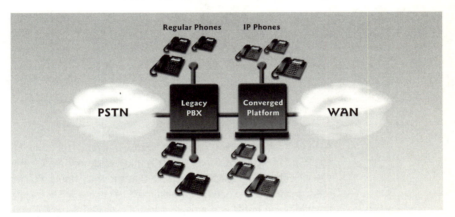

Figure 3.5.: *Converged platforms enable interworking with legacy PBXs. This allows IP Communications to be introduced and evaluated at departmental level or in one or more remote locations.*

Converged platforms can connect to the public telephone network directly or, as shown here, they can interface to a legacy PBX. If both systems come from the same vendor then the two circuit-switched elements function as if they were one system. The legacy phones can remain in place or they can be connected to the new platform, as can the new IP phones. The IP devices could, for example, be initially deployed in one or more departments, those that would benefit most from the new functionality.

Converged platforms are therefore an ideal way to trial the concept and evaluate the benefits. In addition, they are a useful way of adding capacity to a legacy PBX and to protect legacy investments during the transition period.

More IP phones can be added in line with the success of the trial and when the time comes to replace the legacy system then, as shown in figure 3.6, the converged platform can take over its phones and cabling.

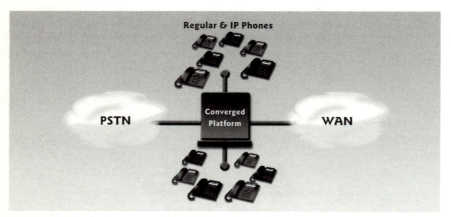

Figure 3.6.: *When the time comes to replace the PBX, regular phones continue to be used by employees who do not require the additional functionality.*

A mixed circuit/packet switched scenario would typically be employed in locations where all the employees do not require the new IP-enhanced applications. Note that the trial should also be used to evaluate the network, which must be engineered to handle the additional traffic and provide a high Quality of Service (QoS). QoS is a fundamental attribute of converged networks that support business applications.

Converged platforms do enable graceful migration to IP Communications, but since we are moving towards an all-IP environment one can question the wisdom of retaining the legacy phones. The main argument is financial. Giving everybody a new IP phone represents a significant investment: these devices currently cost between $150 and $400, so they are only going to be given to the employees who will profit the most from the new functionality. Prices will come down in line with market growth, so that is another reason for delaying widespread implementation.

Regular phones as well as other analog devices such as cordless DECT phones and facsimile machines can continue to function in an all-IP environment. In this case they interoperate via adapters.

The vendors of the new systems would obviously like to sell as many new desktop phones as possible, but it is worth considering the potential of softphones as cost-effective alternatives. This is an important subject and it is covered in some detail in chapter four.

Native IP platforms

A native IP platform is one that only employs packet switching. Other terms are: IP PBX, LAN PBX and softswitch. Sales of these systems are growing rapidly, albeit from a small base, but parity with PBXs is expected around 2005/6 and by the end of the decade circuit switched systems will no longer be employed in corporate networks. Converged platforms are therefore an elegant and cost-effective way of making the transition to the new environment.

Both data- and voice-centric vendors market native IP platforms. Converged platforms come from the voice side of the voice-data equation.

This book does not seek to take sides in the voice-data convergence debate, but one cannot ignore the fact that there are two sides: one is voice centric and it comes from the vendors of PBXs; the other is data centric and it comes from the vendors of IP equipment. There was an early war of words about the respective merits of these two camps and they can be summarized in a semi-serious joke: one side had to learn how to spell IP and the other had to learn how to spell reliability. The debate is now more serious and there is broad agreement about the overall objective, that of having an all-IP information and communications infrastructure. However, as one would expect, there are significant differences about the best way to get there and the timetable.

Data-centric vendors pioneered softswitches and were the first to market with IP Communications solutions. Their portfolio does not include converged platforms. The voice-centric vendors were obviously aware that IP was the future but had to protect their mainstream business and the installed base, i.e. come up with a migration strategy other than that of a forklift upgrade. Converged platforms form part of that strategy.

There are circumstances in which the forklift upgrade approach can be justified, e.g. an organization has a number of PBXs that have come to the end of their life cycles and/or a number of new locations need to be added to the corporate network. Adding new locations is a relatively simple task, particularly when IP Communications has been implemented at one or more central sites, but the physical replacement of PBXs and their phones by IP platforms and new phones is fundamentally distruptive. It can be accomplished quite quickly, but not over a weekend, so the new telephony system will normally be implemented off line and will run in parallel with the legacy system before being cut over.

Having covered converged platforms in some detail, we should point out that a native IP switch can interoperate with a legacy PBX via a gateway, as shown in figure 3.7. The end result is similar, one obvious difference being the fact that IP phones are the only devices that can connect directly to the new system. Analog phones and other devices connect via adapters.

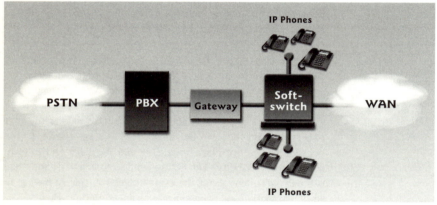

Figure 3.7.: Softswitches, which are native IP platforms, connect to PBXs (and the PSTN) via gateways.

It is impossible to say which way works best and decisions should not be taken on the respective merits of the two architectures. Apart from cost and confidence, many other factors have to be taken into consideration, but the two most important aspects of IP Communications are the applications and the functionality of the phone. What applications does the vendor offer as part of the solution and how open is that solution to third-party developers. This subject was covered in earlier chapters. The functionality of the phone is covered in Chapter 4, but voice-centric vendors are able to deliver hundreds of features — that is part of their core competence. Data-centric vendors question the need for more than say 30 features.

Capex comparisons

Forrester Research has produced a white paper that makes cost comparisons between five migration strategies. These are:

- Keep an existing PBX
- Replace PBX with another PBX
- Replace PBX with an IP PBX (Softswitch)
- Replace PBX with an IP converged system within a competitive environment
- Migration of an existing PBX to an IP converged system.

Forrester's calculation is based on a customer scenario involving 10,000 users, half of whom work at two large locations and the remainder at twelve branch offices. Other assumptions: 100 million minutes of national long distance traffic a year, 20% of which are internal; 1 million internal minutes, 40% of which are internal. This model also incorporated research conducted by InfoTech into the projected phone mix by 2005. Assumptions here include: a company migrating to an IP converged system will keep 63% of the existing phones; when investing in an IP PBX 17% of the analog devices will need to be integrated (e.g. faxes); Only 15% of the users within an IP PBX and 9% of the users within an IP converged environment will use an IP soft client by 2005. (The authors think that figure will rise when the market realizes that soft phones complement regular phones; they are not foreseen as replacements.)

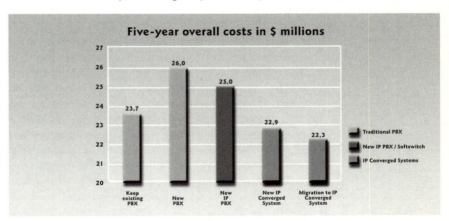

Figure 3.8.: The financial calculations are based on the above assumptions plus the capex and five-year operating costs. Thus, keeping the existing PBXs would not result in additional capital costs.

Note that these figures do not include the impact on the bottom line of the new applications, e.g. the significant increase in productivity. Thus, the total cost of keeping an existing PBX or replacing it with a new PBX is much higher. The lowest overall cost comes when the company migrates to an IP converged system. Why is this the case? According to Forrester the integration of analog devices as well as the need for analog public network support within an IP PBX through analog adapters and gateways is significantly more expensive than that of a converged platform, which includes a circuit-switched interface.

Paths to convergence

The authors have identified six common approaches to convergence:

1) The Quantum Leap

Some organizations will make the jump to 100% packet-switched solutions. These tend to be risk-tolerant organizations that favor leading-edge solutions and many will be technology companies themselves. However, they will also buy some insurance by pairing a circuit switch with the packet switch and using gateways to access the public infrastructure.

2) Apps-In

Other organizations will start by moving to convergence at the applications layer and then work their way in towards the network. In this approach the convergence of voice and data, both wireline and wireless, becomes part of sophisticated unified communication solutions that function within a circuit switched infrastructure. Thus, this approach leverages the systems that are already in place. Application examples include multi-media customer contact centers and corporate GSM. These and other apps deliver convergence at the application layer today and in future they can be migrated to a packet-switched environment.

3) Edge-In

One of the most compelling convergence solutions today is based on the connection of edge sites and users via IP. Enterprise-class IP networking is considerably cheaper than networks that employ E1/T1 links or leased lines. Moreover, the edge-in approach enables users at remote sites to share applications, have centralized administration, and enjoy transparent dialing and features. For many enterprises, this enables connectivity and resource sharing at small sites that was cost prohibitive in the circuit-switched world.

4) Evolution

Mature technologies don't have a lot of bugs. They've been worked out over time, but even the best new technologies can take a while before they can be rated as robust. The evolutionary approach to convergence is one in which the organization evaluates optimal risk/performance points throughout the enterprise and uses a mix of circuit and packet-switched solutions to meet the needs of individuals, workgroups, locations and the enterprise as a whole. It is a good way to implement point solutions and then enhance them at a later date.

5) Outsourcing

With outsourcing, the vendor carries the risk and deploys the solutions that deliver the right functionality, with the best service level for the best price. This will, for most enterprises, ultimately mean at least some packet-switched communications, particularly for multi-site enterprises, with a growing use of IP over time. Look for vendors who offer rigorous service level agreements.

6) Exploration

Packet switching changes many things in the communications environment. Network managers need to get used to the rigors of real time applications and the networks need to be upgraded, e.g. QoS mechanisms introduced. A new level of diagnostic capability is also required. User features accomplish the same things as in a circuit- switched world, but they must accomplish these differently. All enterprises should be trialing convergence solutions now to gain skills and understand how and when their technology buying strategies should shift.

The new environment

Figure 3.9 represents a converged voice-data environment. We have renamed the softswitch: it is now a communications server, since this is a better reflection of its role in a client-server model. Some IP telephony applications will reside in this platform; other applications

• Migration: the #1 issue

will be hosted in one or more application servers. Note that the communications platform can be a converged platform as well as a native IP switch. IP phones have two ports; one connects to the LAN switch and the other to the workstation. Both are client devices that work in client-server modes. Databases and data applications are hosted in regular computer servers.

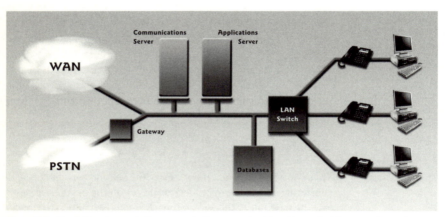

Figure 3.9.: *An all-IP environment. The communications server handles call control while a second server hosts the applications. Mainstream processes such as the CRM database can be communications enabled.*

We can now see — literally — how voice-data convergence works. There is no more computer telephony glue; voice and data are transported over the same network and they employ the same communications protocol. And since voice is now another data type it can be processed and manipulated in any way that makes commercial sense.

Recall what was said earlier about IP's intrinsic flexibility. If you log onto your corporate network from any location in the world you will immediately have access to all authorized applications and new email will be delivered automatically. There is no need to tell the system where you are: your new IP address is allocated dynamically as soon as you log in and identify yourself to the network. That is something we take for granted when it comes to data. This is a revolutionary concept when applied to voice; PBXs are location-centric systems; in an IP environment locations are irrelevant.

This ability to access and share communications resources over the wide area network means that remote offices and individual users do not need a local switching capability. All that is needed is a switch/router and broadband access to the nearest point of presence. Thus, the Internet takes over the role of the local loop — the connection to the nearest public switch in regular telephony — and Internet access is ubiquitous.

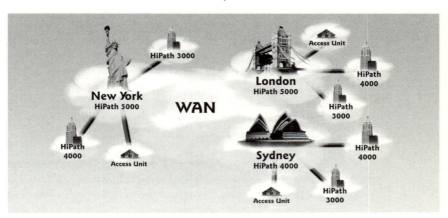

Figure 3.10.: *Relatively large softswitches will normally be installed at one or more large sites, e.g. regional headquarters. IP applications will be hosted at these sites and can be used by any authorized employee from any location on the network.*

Enterprise-wide networks will evolve in different ways, but there is a generic topology. As shown in figure 3.10, Relatively large, native IP platforms will be located at the company's main offices, e.g. two per continent, one on the West coast and one on the East coast in the case of the US. The IP applications will be hosted at these sites. Medium sized offices will have smaller switching platforms, the size will depend on the number of local employees, and the network will be used to access the applications. Other locations may have a small platform or simply a router/switch. A single person only needs a router; a small office of say 3-4 employees would typically have a small LAN and in those cases a router/switch would be used.

The inherent flexibility of this type of network indicates that new offices can come on stream in a few hours and access to every application is enabled at the same time. A physical call center is no longer required; this is just another application and the agents can be anywhere; specialists can even be mobile.

Conclusions

IP-enabled telephony turns voice into what is virtually a new media type yet at the same time nothing changes; for example, a mobile/cellular phone can be used to access and process email but it's still a regular phone. Telephony functions are embedded in the infrastructure; they are a centralised resource that is managed centrally, but at the same time the architecture of the new infrastructure is intrinsically flexible. IP Communications therefore represents a mix of revolutionary concepts, amazing functionality and common sense. This development cuts costs, boosts productivity, reduces transaction costs, hones competitive edges and makes a significant and immediate impact on the bottom line.

The business case could hardly be more compelling and there are any number of pragmatic migration scenarios that will take you from today to tomorrow along a route that matches your individual requirements at each and every step.

CHAPTER FOUR
Phones, PDAs, and their amazing new functionality

This chapter considers the hands-on experience of IP Communications. What is the look and feel of the new telephony interface; how do PCs enable easy use of advanced functionality and how do phones and PCs function as a single entity? In addition, it examines the role of wireless communications in the office environment and 'hot spots'.

IP Phones may look like regular devices, others have relatively large screens and some feature a color display. Larger screens enable more information to be displayed and this facilitates use of 'thin-client' applications. This term is used to describe a device that has similar functionality to a PC but which employs fewer resources, e.g. a PDA is a thin-client device. Employees who do not require a desktop PC for their work can use one of these large-screen phones for data

Pen Tablet and IP Phone. Photos courtesy of Fujitsu-Siemens (left) and Avaya (right)

• Phones, PDAs, and their amazing new functionality

tasks, e.g. to access directories and other corporate information published on the intranet. These devices employ menu-driven graphical interfaces and have other PC-type features such as the ability to search the corporate directory and set up personal directories. In addition, IP phones will normally have flash memory in order to facilitate software upgrades. Large screens make it easier to employ the more advanced telephone features such as conference calls and these devices also simplify the provisioning of multimedia contact center agents capable of handling voice calls, emails and interactive Web calls.

The software that drives IP phones can be downloaded to a PC or PDA, which allows these devices to be used as so-called softphones. This enables use of a much bigger screen and more powerful computing resources. One may be forgiven for being somewhat underwhelmed at the idea of using a PC as a phone, more on this in a moment, but the real objective is to create a best-of-both worlds scenario, i.e. to use PC/PDA resources to complement those of the phone. For example, instead of using top-of-the-range models having large color displays, a basic phone can be employed and the PC used to set up personal directories and employ advanced telephony features such as conference calls. Alternatively, a telephony handset can be connected to the USB of the PC. These devices look like a stripped down phone; there is no display or keypad. They cost around $100. An obvious disadvantage is the need for the PC to be switched on; if it is off no calls can be received or made.

A notebook PC or PDA that has been configured as a softphone can also be used as a phone when mobile. In order to make and receive calls a connection to the corporate network via the Internet is required, e.g. a wireless 'hot spot' such as an airport lounge.

In future the way people work will depend on their needs and locations; they will not be limited by the functionality of the devices. PDAs will function in combination with cellular phones; they can also be employed as a phone. Videoconferencing could take place on the notebook or PDA while the phone is used to talk. Files can be shared and changes made by mobile colleagues while they continue to talk. Calls will be automatically forwarded to wireless when out of the office and routed back to wireline when one enters the office again. These benefits derive from IP's intrinsic flexibility and the SIP standard.

The combination of a large screen, a graphical display and powerful computing resources brings a totally new dimension to telephony. In the following example of a softphone interface the frequently called parties are identified using icons or photos, and telephony features such as call forward, transfer and conference call are invoked

Phones, PDAs, and their amazing new functionality •

by dragging an icon or picture to the relevant part of the screen. In the case of conference calls, which is the application shown here, participants are invited by dragging and dropping directory entries into the communications circle.

The story may be apocryphal, but on seeing this interface a prospective customer asked if it would be possible to drag and drop participants into the trash bin.

This drag and drop process creates a virtual conference room and once the voice conference has been established, the participants can go on to share the applications running on the different desktops. Note that the PC's more powerful resources are employed to facilitate communications; after setting up a conference call or using the PC to access a corporate directory the IP phone is used for the actual conversation.

Graphical interfaces enable advanced telephony functions such as conference calls to be set up in seconds simply by dragging icons into the conference circle at the center. Recall how presence flags are used to check on availability and how instant messaging can be used to schedule conferences.

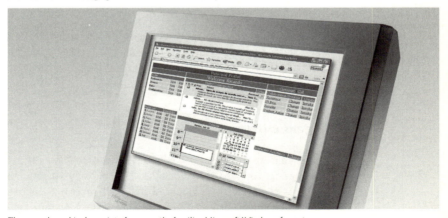

The second graphical user interface uses the familiar Microsoft Windows format.

85 •

Telephony features

PBX vendors have spent many years developing a very comprehensive portfolio of telephony features for end users, e.g. caller list, call back, recall, do-not-disturb, override, hunt group, group call, etc., etc. In addition, as one would expect, all major public networking standards are supported. While this is mandatory because of the obvious need to interoperate with the PSTN and the PBXs of other vendors, one can query the actual usage of the many telephony features on offer. A typical user may only use a dozen or so features from a portfolio of a few hundred, but different users use different features and user groups and vertical industries have specialized requirements. PBX vendors are therefore obliged to port as many features as possible to their IP platforms and softphone interfaces, as we have seen, facilitate usage. Thus, functionality that was not used on the regular phone may be employed in the new IP environment.

Vendors who come from the data side of the computer telephony equation do not attempt to compete in this area and will typically offer around 30 features. This is more than adequate for most users, but if your company does require some of those special telephony features it might be an issue.

Microsoft Outlook and Lotus Notes are data applications, and unified messaging comes via the addition of voicemail to these inboxes.

There has been a traditional voice versus data side to IP communications and it was preceded by the earlier unidirectional approach to computer telephony integration (CTI). CTI applications such as unified messaging and call centers basically involved the integration of telephony features with a data application. Put another way, real time communications was merely an addition.

The end-user experience is that of a single messaging application, but it is realized via the integration of separate systems.

IP enables a bidirectional approach. As we saw in chapter two, a data application such as instant messaging can be integrated with telephony in order to indicate availability and phone functionality can be employed on a PC or PDA.

IP goes wireless

IP Communications leverages a company's investment in local and wide area networks; so does Wireless LAN technology. This started out life as a data-centric development and its relevance to telephony may not be immediately obvious, but when voice is another data type the same wireless access method can be employed.

W-LAN solutions use unlicensed spectrum so no operators are involved. Small base stations connect to the LAN as shown in figure 6.1, and these communicate with wireless client devices. These are notebook PCs and PDAs that have the requisite wireless interface. In most cases this is provided by a PC card that slots into the device, but this access method has been built into many new notebook PCs, i.e. it is there by default.

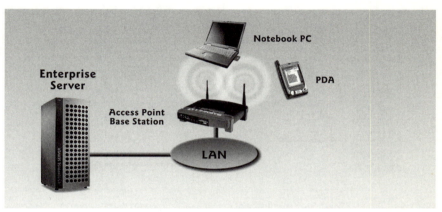

Figure 4.1.: *Small base stations on the LAN convert the wireless data traffic into IP for transmission over the corporate infrastructure.*

Unfortunately, W-LAN systems ship with the baseline security feature turned off and this resulted in negative media coverage.

Security can be enhanced via proprietary solutions, but a new standard has been finalized and it will be implemented by all leading vendors.

The base stations convert the wireless signal into IP so that it can be sent over the LAN, thereby allowing the wireless data devices to communicate with host resources. This is a particularly useful facility for employees who are mobile, e.g. salespeople can enter any corporate office and get immediate access to their email. Wireless enabled notebooks are also employed when mobile within the office. They can be carried to other offices and the wireless link to the LAN is retained; hosted files can be downloaded for use at meetings and documents exchanged between participants. These solutions have become very popular, which has driven down the price of base stations and PC cards; in fact, small base stations for SMBs and home users have become commodity items.

Compatibility between the PC cards and base stations of different vendors was an early issue, but this has been resolved. This task is handled by the Wireless Ethernet Compatibility Alliance (Details at: www.wi-fi.com), which brands compliant products as "Wi-Fi." The term Wi-Fi is now used generically, i.e. it refers to the wireless LAN access method.

• Phones, PDAs, and their amazing new functionality

Wireless voice

A niche market has developed on the voice side of Wi-Fi. Phones that use the same air interface have been developed and as illustrated in figure 6.2, they communicate with their own base stations and a communications server sets up calls between devices.

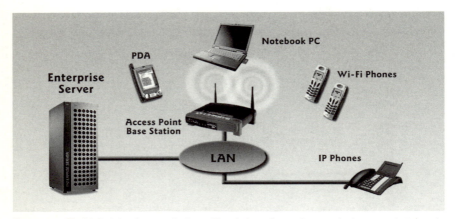

Figure 4.2.: *The Wi-Fi air interface can also be used for telephony. A second communications server (not shown) is needed for call control.*

In this case the base stations convert the wireless signals into VoIP. This enables calls to travel across the LAN/WAN until they reach the relevant base station, i.e. the nearest one to the called party. These solutions have been employed in hospitals and warehouses, and for the latter application wireless PDAs are used for tasks such as inventory.

SIPing into the picture

The data transfer rates of 11 and 50 Mbps refer to the maximum speed of the air interface. Actual end-user rates depend on the number of users in the hot spot.

The deployment of the Wi-Fi solution in business locations such as airport lounges, conference centers, hotels and even coffee shops is a very logical development. These locations are known as 'hot spots'. Transmission rates are close to that of the wireline LAN (11 Mbps rising to 50 Mbps) and more than adequate for a mobile professional's requirements. Hot spots represent a low capex investment; they meet a market need, so they are being implemented at a staggering rate.

We also indicated that notebook PCs and the more advanced PDAs can be used as softphones and they can also have wireless interfaces.

In addition, SIP software can be added in order set up a session (communications link) with the IP platform.

Employees of organizations that have implemented IP Communications can set up SIP-enabled sessions from these hot spots. They connect via the Internet to the corporate network's nearest point of presence (PoP) and then they can talk to any other phone in the world. Thus, they are using a voice-enabled PDA or a notebook PC as if it was a regular cellular/mobile phone but there is a big difference: the cost. The regular backbone network that is employed for international mobile calls has been bypassed and this part of the journey is free. If the call is to a colleague then the only charge is that of the hot spot and access is not metered, so any number of calls can be made.

Hot spot tariffs are only just emerging, but they are very economic and in many cases access is free, e.g. in the business lounges of international airports. This development will obviously impact on the revenues of mobile network operators but they are rising to the challenge in a positive way. For example, subscribers would obviously like to be billed for hot spot access in the same way as voice, i.e. international data roaming should be enabled and everything should be itemized on the same bill at the end of the month. In addition, rather than fighting toll bypass — a battle that cannot be won — they are likely to embrace systems that facilitate access to local corporate PoPs in order to help retain valuable corporate accounts.

GSM in the office

In the past various wireless network vendors promoted 'GSM in the office' solutions. The basic idea was to encourage extended use of these phones within the wireline office environment by reducing the cost of internal wireless communications. Internal calls had become a problem because the mobile section of the workforce had become so used to making calls to colleagues on their GSM phone that they were phoning each other over the air when both parties were in the same office. Corporate phone bills were therefore inflated by use of this relatively expensive medium.

This vendor-centric concept did not fly for various reasons, one being the premise that operators would allow GSM spectrum to be used in the designated area(s) for a flat fee, i.e. calls within the

• Phones, PDAs, and their amazing new functionality

office are therefore not metered. In addition, the idea of having pico cells on office walls was not appealing. However, the rationale of only using one phone is sound and the more mobile the workforce the sounder it becomes.

A more recent development was the idea of a 'mini' GSM system for enterprises and one such system has been implemented by a major Scandinavian car manufacturer. This has all the requisite functionality but would be cheaper because scaling to carrier levels would not be needed; in addition it featured IP conversion. Thus, cells were physically mounted on the wall but virtually they lived on the LAN. Unfortunately GSM operators were still concerned about loss of revenue so flat-fee access hit the deck and in this case that concern had global implications: wireless calls made over the WAN would bypass the international tollgates.

Businesses would clearly welcome a development that cut down the cost of communicating and a phone that had two air interfaces — cellular and Wi-Fi — would be a neat solution. However, these phones are unlikely to hit the market in the foreseeable future (a) because of Bluetooth and (b) the problem can be solved at source by using a virtual phone instead of a physical device. The latter development is covered in the next section.

The voice side of Bluetooth technology tends to get overlooked. It is primarily seen as a short-range wireless interface for data applications such as the synchronization between mobile and desktop machines, e.g. PDAs and PCs. It is also used in personal area networks. However, you can also use Bluetooth to build up wireless networks that enable office connectivity along the lines outlined earlier. Bluetooth-enabled GSM phones link to access points that live on the LAN and these are used to convert signals to VoIP. This solution is therefore similar to those that employ Wi-Fi. The Bluetooth interface is used for internal communications and GSM elsewhere. You need network management software to get everything to work and a gateway to enable communications over the PSTN, but this development work has been done.

How does the phone know which air interface to use? That would have been a tricky issue but these new phones default to the Bluetooth air interface and if this signal is not present they switch over to GSM. Thus, when mobile workers enter the office the phone will be locked onto the Bluetooth signal that is transmitted by the access points. If the GSM phone of a colleague is rung and this person is also locked onto Bluetooth then the call will go over the LAN/WAN, i.e. the cellular network will have been bypassed 100%.

Unfortunately there is a downside. In addition to the cost of implementing this type of solution the mobile workforce will have to be equipped with new phones.

A lateral leap

Using the corporate infrastructure to bypass that of the mobile network operator makes sense. Why pay for a wireless call when both parties are inside the same building or on the same campus site? However, solutions that only address the financial issue are missing out in other areas, one of which is the need to enable IT departments to monitor and control wireless telephony. In other words, to make it part of the new voice-data environment.

Wireless telephony is scheduled to go IP; that is part of 3G's promise, but quite apart from the uncertainty about actual implementation the investment in 2G circuit-switched phones is massive. Thus, voice-data convergence along the same lines as wireline telephony is out of the question.

This development removes the need for a separate, point solution and it underlines the earlier point about synergistic relationships between applications and the huge benefits that result when there is no need to reinvent the same communications wheel.

The lateral leap that we invite you to take involves revisiting the concept of presence. This groundbreaking application is premised on the use of a single virtual number that callers use. If the called party has logged onto the network the system will ring the wireline phone; if there is no answer or if the party has not logged on the mobile phone will be rung. Thus, unnecessary use of mobiles is eliminated at source because nobody dials those numbers: only the virtual number is employed.

Work done in the Parlay Group also recognizes the need for similar control to that of wireline telephony, for example, the ability to bar international calls outside regular office hours for certain employees and to centralize costs.

The ability to monitor and control wireless telephony comes via work done in the Parlay Group, which is an open multi-vendor consortium formed to develop open, technology-independent APIs. Here are some key phrases from the Group's charter: "to generate and provide products and/or services that use the functionality resident in existing networks ... aims to create an explosion in the number of communication applications by specifying and promoting open APIs that link IT applications with the capabilities of the communications world."

These APIs will be used to develop many next-generation applications and a key enabler will be the ability to enable interoperation between public networks (wireline and wireless) and private networks such as those of enterprises. In the case of wireless telephony presence, availability and location are three network parameters that are known to the network. Use of these mobile parameters will be conditional on a business arrangement, but it will allow a call made to a mobile number to be redirected to another device. For example, if the system sees that the called party's location is that of the office then it can be sent to the wireline phone. Thus, the functionality is very similar to that of an enterprise that has implemented a solution based on the use of a single virtual number. The latter is available now, the former is a near- to medium-term delivery.

Conclusions

The boundaries between wireline and wireless communications are set to disappear along the lines indicated earlier. Communications and computing will become ubiquitous, enabling seamless roaming in and out of different networks: wireline office to Wi-Fi office, Wi-Fi to 2.5 G cellular; 2.5G to Wi-Fi in hot spots, back to 2.5G and then Wi-Fi again in the home. Moreover, the same secure connection is retained. Mobile professionals will make increasing use of multi-modal PDAs (text, voice and eventually video) having multi-modal air interfaces (Bluetooth, Wi-Fi and 2.5G).

Devices will have automatic associations. The phone appears to be part of the PC and the PC part of the phone. When the PC is on, keys on the phone function as extensions of the PC. Instant messages appear on the screen of the phone as well as the presence and availability icons. The same information will be displayed on Wi-Fi devices so the same functionality can be employed when users are away from their desk. Presence and availability can also be seen from remote hot spots. Cellular calls made by corporate employees will be redirected to the nearest point of presence, thereby enabling the corporate network to be used for long distance and international wireless telephony. And this is just the beginning — the emerging tip of the IP communications iceberg.

CHAPTER FIVE
Video enters the picture

In this final chapter we look at the deployment and benefits of Video over IP. This is a relatively easy media type to add to a converged network, the key parameter being bandwidth, which is not an issue. Video is being used to enhance desktop meetings and facilitate the use of this medium for international conferences, thereby minimizing the need to travel and attend 'in person'. However, the biggest benefit will probably turn out to be the ability to add this real time media type when collaborating.

In the executive summary we pointed out that voice is a very rich medium, that the human voice is the best way to convey subtle messages, to express feelings and emotions; it is also the optimum way to reach consensus on difficult issues. However, in recent years email has become the primary medium for business communications because it is cheap and effective — ideal for working over time zones and in carrying attachments that would once have been faxed. But there are no shades of meaning in emails and misunderstandings can arise. Thus, we need to use a combination of real time 'human' media and electronic enhancements. Long-distance and international telephony tariffs have come down significantly in recent years, so cost is not a significant issue, but video has been out of the financial reach of many companies.

IP Telephony is taking voice back to its communications future. This real-time media type can now be used to complement instant messaging (IM) and email as we have seen in earlier chapters. Clicking on an IM screen 'pop' that asks if you are free to talk, for example, will set up the call immediately. Moreover, the ability to manage one's presence increases the effectiveness of telephony since more

• Video enters the picture

In future, when video comes to corporate desktops, video will be employed as the next best thing to a face-to-face meeting and we can anticipate increased use of this medium when usage increases and it becomes something we take for granted.

calls get through first time. The next step is obvious: add the visual element when you want to replicate a meeting and/or enhance collaboration. Seeing the people to whom you are talking enhances communications even though something like 90% of the content is speech based. Images, pictures and video play an important role in personal relationships and they complement and enhance the spoken word, which in turn enhances email and facsimile.

As shown in figure 5.1, one can visualize this relationship. Email is ideal for routine work and when decisions can be taken without a discussion. When text-based is not up to the task and personal involvement is needed phones are currently employed.

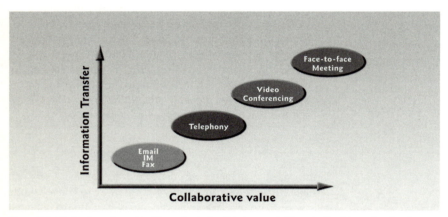

Figure 5.1: *Electronic media are ideal for routing tasks. Telephony and video enter the picture when there is a need for personal involvement.*

Video tracking voice

ISDN is a well-established digital telecommunications standard. It enables data to be transported at rates of between 128 kbps and 2 Mbps, which is low by today's standards. ISDN is based on circuit-switched technology and is expensive compared to packet-switched services.

In the last decade the enterprise telephony network has continued to evolve, enabling voice communications to continue to increase its efficiency, functionality, and simplicity as it migrates to an IP-based paradigm. Now we are seeing the same trend in video communications. Videoconferencing technology has migrated from legacy ISDN (Integrated Services Digital Network) to a fully converged IP network; enterprises are able to not only reduce their network access costs by eliminating costly ISDN connections but also deliver video communication and video collaboration tools to enterprise desktops.

Video communication, with voice and data, may be used for multiple applications using either meeting rooms that have dedicated equipment or an end-user desktop environment. For example:

- Conferences; as a replacement to face-to-face meeting
- Collaboration; desktop-based data collaboration and converged communications among two or more users
- Distance learning; enables the training of multiple people in multiple locations
- Telemedicine; enables consultation, second opinion and remote healthcare.
- Finance; investor relations, video teller
- Engineering; design teams.

However, before examining the benefits of video conferencing and video communications in the enterprise over a converged IP network, we should take a brief look at the evolution of the network and recent changes in technology.

Videoconferencing has been around since the mid-1960s but its deployment within enterprises did not start until the '80s and even then it was only affordable by large corporations. Systems were proprietary and expensive and until that time the networks could not handle the data requirements. Video consumes vast amounts of bandwidth; at ten frames a second the total bandwidth requirement is 16 Mbps and this is one of the reasons why a new network, the ISDN, was designed and implemented. However, compression and other techniques had to be developed in order to bring the bandwidth requirement down without impacting on picture quality.

Unfortunately high-quality video transmission could only be achieved using multiple ISDN channels, but even so many companies decided that value of the medium exceeded the cost. However, all attempts to roll out ISDN to the desktop failed. ATM (Asynchronous Transfer Mode), a telecommunications technology that followed ISDN, was packet-based and ideal for real time voice and video. However, just as it was maturing to the point of taking off and being implemented on corporate networks, IP came onto the scene and the rest, as they say, is history. Video over IP is now not only enabling cost-effecting solutions for video conferencing, but it is also facilitating the delivery of video to the desktop.

• Video enters the picture

IP's impact

The cost of video conferencing comes down significantly when an IP service replaces leased lines and once again we see the intrinsic flexibility of IP Communications. Implementing Video over IP is a logical next step for many companies. It leverages the same LAN/WAN infrastructure, thereby improving the ROI, and for desktop meetings the systems upgrade cost is minimal. The information and communications network must be engineered to handle the additional traffic and this is something that should be evaluated at an early stage, ideally before the move to IP telephony. This will help ensure a smooth transition at a later date.

Voice gets the gold service, video the silver and data the bronze.

At first sight it would seem that video places higher demands on the infrastructure and the delivery mechanisms, but this is not the case: telephony is the critical media type. Both voice and video are influenced by delay and jitter, but the spoken word is the key component. If conversations start to break up, something that happens all too frequently with cellular telephony, user dissatisfaction will kick in very quickly. However, if the picture freezes slightly from time to time the impact on the communications process is minimal and it might not be noticed. Thus, while IP networks have priority mechanisms that give priority to voice over data, as we have seen in earlier chapters, they are now used to give secondary priority to video over IP.

This application will typically run in client-server mode, the server taking care of the registration of clients in an online telephone directory and in at least one case, the solution also manages the network bandwidth allocation for group conferences. As well as being used for distributed project teams, real time collaboration might involve customers and prospects.

Video is a relatively new medium, but at the same time it is very natural way to communicate and one can therefore anticipate fast acceptance by end users and a further reduction in transaction costs via the increase in productivity.

The business case for moving onwards and upwards, from voice over IP to video over IP, is clear. When video is available at all relevant desktops it will be employed, particularly by users who are collaborating on one or more projects. And we can expect to see a number of software enhancements to be developed and marketed in the near term. For example, systems will detect who is talking and display the relevant head and shoulders shot in the desktop window. This facility is employed in professional videoconferencing systems.

As discussed in earlier chapters, Instant Messaging, Presence and Web Conferencing are additional "media" types that enhance the communication experience. Calls may start with voice and users can add in other media and proceeding to voice and video communication or go direct to a full audio/visual conference. This type of enhancement is impossible on regular voice or data networks. However the true benefits are not only in infrastructure. By moving video communication to an IP-based architecture users will also be able to converge video with a multitude of collaboration applications, both in the meeting room and to the desktop.

Videoconferencing versus desktop video

The term 'conference' in 'videoconference' indicates the relatively formal nature of the medium, i.e. groups of people gather together around two or more systems at a prearranged time. Usually, special scheduling programs are used to set the meeting and reserve resources. Desktop meetings are more informal (ad-hoc); in this case the term indicates that people comfortably remain in front of their own PC's. This kind of meeting could be initiated via instant messages and once again presence management comes into play. A group member who wants to start a discussion could start with a check on the availability of the other members; an instant message would then be sent if a sufficient number were free and the discussion might even start this way. Audio and video would then be added in order to make the discussion more personal and more productive.

Although the baseline technology is the same, video conferencing and desktop meetings have different requirements. The key objective of the former is to minimize the need for face-to-face meetings, particularly those involving international travel. The financial and time savings (time is also money) are significant and rather obvious, but there are other important benefits. Attendees tend to be better prepared for video conferences, possibly because the association of high communications costs lingers on. And they can be conducted with matching teams.

Many international meetings comprise one or two people who travel to the meeting and may be tired when they arrive. Across the table a team that represents different disciplines, e.g. marketing, research, engineering and manufacturing, will often confront them. Thus, the meeting is inevitably skewed towards the home side. In a

• Video enters the picture

video conference experts from the different disciplines can drop in and out of the meeting on both sides: engineers talk to engineers, scientists to scientists and so on. A better balance is achieved and as a result better decisions can be taken.

Video conferences can also be set up quickly since no travel is involved, which makes the medium particularly effective for crisis situations. People can also be brought in from different locations even though attendance may only be needed for a short time. In the past companies would often attend meetings with a team in tow and all too often the contribution of specialists would be minimal or even zero. Nevertheless they had to be there in case they were needed.

Thus, the key benefits are:

- Reduced travel budgets and reduced travel time
- Better meetings; optimal balance, e.g. between headquarters and a manufacturing location
- Rapid access to specialists
- More meetings, but shorter.

The benefits of desktop meetings

Desktop video is an informal application and as indicated earlier, it will be used to enhance phone conversations, both one-on-one and in workgroup discussions. Unlike conferencing, the screen display

Photo courtesy of Logitech.

Figure 5.2: *Webcams are used by PC enthusiasts because of the low price plus the fact that the software is free, i.e. NetMeeting is bundled with the Microsoft's desktop operating systems.*

will be much smaller, which reduces bandwidth requirements, and pictures will be captured via small, desktop cameras, which are often mounted on top of the monitor. The popular term for these devices is Webcam and they typically cost US $50-150. Web indicates that the vision they capture can be seen over the Internet, e.g. traffic situations. Engineers, particularly those that collaborate with each other from different locations, also employ these devices and Net-Meeting software.

Real time collaboration

Real time collaboration is an application that comes between the rather basic desktop meeting described in the previous section and a full-blown video conference. It would typically start with a check on awareness, be followed by instant text messages and then a chat session. Participants could then move on, adding audio and video to make the session more personal. As shown in the following screen shot, communications software running in different windows enables availability information to be displayed as well as contact lists (aka buddy lists). Simply dragging names into the window that contains the communications application can start audio and video conferencing. Documents and other files can be exchanged in a similar way.

Figure 5.3.: *This window within Windows shows how a collaboration session that starts with IM or telephony can add video in order to enhance and improve the communications process.*

Video will also be used across time zones. Both voice and video collaborative sessions can be recorded and shared off-line, with

• Video enters the picture

'markers' that indicate critical areas such as those where there is a major disagreement or when a decision has been taken. Other parties can fast-forward to these areas in order to capture the feeling of the discussion and if they wish to comment then annotations can be introduced and the new version circulated around the group. This process is employed when documents such as systems descriptions are created: they are circulated and everybody is free to comment. These sessions can also be archived.

Figure 5.4.: *CEOs and their management teams are not going to mess around (as they would see it) with a Windows application such as NetMeeting. However, there are times when there is no substitute for eye-to-eye contact and that cannot be achieved via a TV in the corner. This is a niche market that a Dutch company is looking to fill.*

The baseline functionality of the video solution shown in figure 5.4 is that of a videophone having a large, high-resolution screen. Called the Eye Catcher, it is designed to provide instant meetings between the top management of multi-location enterprises. These video stations are not cheap: around Euro 25K each, but worth it when you add up executive time and travel costs.

Mobile conferences and meetings

Interactive video is not practical on cellular networks; there is insufficient bandwidth and at best the image would come across as a series of jerky stills. Hot spots, however, are a very different proposition. The current data rate is around 11 Mbps and while the air interface is shared with other users, there would normally be sufficient for displaying pictures on a notebook PC or a powerful PDA.

Video enters the picture •

The data rate is set to move up to a little over 50 Mbps and while the resource is still shared, the bandwidth will start to approach that of a switched LAN, which is 10 Mbps.

Recall one of the key features of hot spots and SIP. Mobile workers in a hot spot employ SIP to set up a remote, secure client-server session. The client device is the notebook or PDA and the server sits on the corporate intranet. This means that there is very little difference in the communications and computing resources; mobile workers have near identical functionality to that of their wireline colleagues.

When collaboration is required and one or more members of the workgroup are mobile they can join the discussion using a cellular phone, or employ the PDA as a phone, and if video is needed they could head for the nearest hot spot, e.g. a Starbucks coffee shop or the business lounge of a city center hotel.

Video broadcasts

IP multicasting allows streaming audio and video to be sent over corporate and public networks while conserving bandwidth.

Companies that make the transition from IP-enhanced voice to IP-enhanced video will be able to benefit in many ways. In addition to video conferencing and desktop meetings, the medium can be used to make remote presentations, to give virtual seminars and marketing updates to key staff, and to 'multicast' messages to thousands of recipients. Files are transmitted over the backbone as a single data stream and subsequently split apart at the end of the path. This technique would allow corporate messages to travel from the headquarters as a single file to regional offices where they would then be split and sent to the individual recipients. IP multicasting is also used for distance learning (aka e-learning), which is the subject of the next chapter.

Conclusions

Talking to moving heads on PC and PDA screens used to be the stuff of science fiction but it is rapidly becoming science fact. No pun intended, but one has to see this medium in action in order to appreciate its convenience and business value. In earlier chapters we saw how telephony and data are merging at both the application and device level; once a well-engineered IP infrastructure is in place and the benefits of IP-enhanced real time telephony have been realized

• Video enters the picture

video can be added to the media mix. Video will be taken for granted and be used as a kind of enhanced version of regular telephony. We do not draw a hard distinction between sounds that enter our ears and the sights that are conveyed to our brains. They are separate senses but the way they are employed is multi-modal and there is no communications interface. At the beginning of the 21st century, and after many technology fast starts, we are close to replicating that experience electronically and economically. The "interesting times" have finally arrived.

Conclusions

This book has indicated the pivotal role that IP convergence and upcoming developments will play in the communications processes of organizations. We have shown how IP-enhanced applications increase productivity by offering more efficient ways of working and indicated the various ways that application 'value chains' enable companies to offer superior customer services to those of the competition. In addition, IP convergence reduces operating costs via lower service costs and easier, simpler network management. The combined result is therefore a very positive impact on the bottom line. Moreover, this development leverages existing investments in current infrastructures (LANs and WAN) and adds functionality to back-office systems such as CRM and ERP. In addition, flexible migration strategies protect legacy investments in PBXs, phones and telephony cabling. IP Communications therefore adds value to the organization and leverages two core assets: human resources and the communications infrastructure. Thus, added value is the key driver behind the implementation of this new communications technology.

The business case for IP convergence is founded on several value principles: (1) the ease with which communications applications can be employed and the speed with which customized applications can be created; (2) the stress-free increase in employee productivity; (3) the faster, better ways of communicating and a reduced need to commute to the office; (4) the ability to respond quickly to changes in the market; (5) the intrinsic flexibility of IP based networks; and (6), the ability to centralize and reduce all communications costs (including mobile calls).

Standards and open systems are driving the deployment of managed IP-centric networks that reduce communications costs significantly. Applications that are easy to use are being developed; in fact, usage is intuitive and one application builds on another to produce personal value chains. And mainstream business processes such as CRM are being communications enabled, which allows companies to deliver superior services.

• Conclusions

Holistic solutions

Point solutions are out; holistic solutions are in. Unified messaging adds a real-time component and becomes unified communications. Customized communications portals carry the concept forward, enabling anywhere, anytime access to all relevant information via a single, secure logon. Instant messaging (online presence) is linked to telephony presence (talking or free). IM chat can morph into telephony via a single mouse click. Presence minimizes telephony tag and facilitates collaboration. Managed availability can be added so that all the important calls get through and others are diverted, e.g. to voicemail. And this is just the start: a today deliverable, the tip of the IP Communications iceberg.

The importance of real time communications is reflected in developments such as Microsoft's operating system component called Greenwich. Greenwich will facilitate real time communications via a set of baseline telephony functions, but these will be enhanced via software extensions that come from the telephony-centric players. This is a necessary and logical development since real time telephony encompasses several hundred functions and features plus a century of operating experience.

Video: the next step

When converged networks are in place and adequately provisioned, Video over IP (the other VoIP) can be added to the communications mix. This is a development that has been long on promise and short on delivery in the past, but a sweet spot is emerging. Bandwidth is not an issue; converged networks enable delivery to the desktop and even mobile devices; NetMeeting is bundled with Microsoft Windows. Thus, it is easy and economic to add the visual element when you want to replicate a meeting and/or enhance collaboration. Video is therefore being used to enhance desktop meetings and minimize the need to travel and attend 'in person'.

Seeing the people to whom you are talking enhances communications even though something like 90% of the content is speech based. Images, pictures and video play an important role in personal relationships and they complement and enhance the spoken word, which in turn enhances email and facsimile.

Changing concepts

The various ways that people work will increasingly depend on their needs and locations; they will not be limited by the functionality of devices. Devices will have automatic associations. The phone becomes part of the PC and the PC part of the phone. When the PC is on, keys on the phone function as extensions of the PC. Instant messages appear on the screen of the phone as well as presence and availability icons. IP-enabled telephony turns voice into what is virtually a new media type yet at the same time nothing changes;

for example, a mobile/cellular phone can be used to access and process email but it's still a regular phone.

Presence and availability can also be seen from remote hot spots. Cellular calls made by corporate employees will be redirected to the nearest point of presence, thereby enabling the corporate network to be used for long distance and international wireless telephony. A videoconference can for example be undertaken on a PDA when mobile. Files can be shared during the conference and changes made in real time.

In addition to the positive impact on the bottom line, which is clearly the single biggest benefit of IP Communications, the book has also demonstrated the graceful way that organizations can migrate from circuit to packet switching. This can be done on a departmental or local office basis in order to trial this paradigm and evaluate the benefits of the new IP-enhanced applications.

Thus, this is a development that adds value to organizations in several ways and there is an attractive return on investment, which ranges from a few months to two years, the average being somewhere in the middle. It is impossible to be more precise since organizations have different requirements and will implement solutions in different ways. This subject is covered in Appendix B and we suggest that you should regard ROIs as a mission-critical product features; they should be part of the solution's specification.

Getting from here to there

The business case for IP Communications is compelling, but migrating to the new environment represents a complex mix of business and technology issues. This is a development that no organization can afford to ignore, but at the same times mistakes could be costly. The technical side of migration was covered in some detail in Chapter 3, but it is clearly impossible to do the same on the business side of the equation since every organization has its own needs and goals. Nevertheless, there is a clear need for the various chief executives, the CxOs, to examine some business fundamentals. For example, what is the overall business strategy and how can Convergence and IP Communications support it? Put another way, you have to know where you want to be before planning the optimal route. Benefits should be quantified and financial returns set against capital and operating costs, i.e. ROIs and TCOs should be evaluated and adjustments made to investment plans if necessary. Ideally this should be done via open discussions with the preferred vendor.

In addition, a move of this importance should be discussed within the organization. It should not be a top-down decision. The various departments and the regional offices will often have a different set of needs and these should be taken into consideration. This might result in an incremental approach, e.g. evaluate the benefits at a department level and them increase the depth and breadth of the implementation within the organization.

• Conclusions

The all-important evaluation process could be based on this simple 5-step 'assess, optimize, and source' approach.

1) **Discover:** gathering the initial data and conducting first assessment and planning executive workshops in order to evaluate gaps, risks, and opportunities. In parallel it is important to obtain executive buy-in and sign-off for the next steps

2) **Executive workshops:** this step runs in parallel with 1)

3) **Assess:** evaluating your current communications infrastructure. The focus is on outlining strategies and recommendations for maximizing communications functionality and reducing total cost of ownership.

4) **Optimize:** designing and implementing technical solutions to fulfill both the business needs and the technical requirements. Optimization is the implementation of the recommendations made in the assess step

5) **Source:** buying the solutions and services at the lowest price and under the terms and conditions that best suit your business.

It's a new communications world that enables new working processes where virtually anything is possible

APPENDIX A
VoIP Services

Organizations having two or more locations will normally interconnect their LANs via a data service. The service provider may be the incumbent carrier, the former PTT whose network was designed to carry regular voice traffic, or one of the new carriers, whose network was originally designed to carry data traffic using frame relay. Details of the frame relay protocol need not concern us, other than to note that it precedes IP and is also based on packet switched technology.

Both the incumbents and the new carriers are now transitioning to IP in order to meet the growing need for VoIP services. The former are seeking to protect their legacy revenue stream; the latter are trying to fill their data pipes with voice traffic. In both cases the baseline offer is that of a VPN (virtual private network).

Baseline VPNs are managed end-to-end by the enterprise. Although the network is a shared resource, a technique known as tunneling makes it virtually private and the addition of IPSec provides high-level security. IPSec is a security protocol that has become the de facto standard for VPNs; it secures everything on the network. When the network is used for voice traffic QoS mechanisms are required in order to give priority to this media type over regular data.

More sophisticated VPNs now allow organizations to hand over the management of the wide area part of the infrastructure to the service provider. In addition, added-value service such as bandwidth on demand and hosted VoIP gateways will be available. Bandwidth in demand eliminates the need to over-provision the network in order to handle peak loads; now you only pay for the resources you actually use. Hosted gateways eliminate the need for this function to be performed at every site in the network.

Hybrid solutions will also be employed. The smaller sites may employ a network-based solution while the remainder will rely on customer premises equipment for end-to-end security. In addition service providers are starting to host IP telephony services and baseline applications such as unified messaging. This is particularly useful for small- and medium-sized businesses since they often lack the resources needed to implement and manage an IP communications solution. An outsourced service can also be used to interconnect tel-

• VoIP Services

eworkers and small offices, i.e. provide a mix and match with the services that are managed internally. However, the kind of productivity enhancing applications such as presence and managed availability are not currently on offer and large organizations will normally want to customize the application portfolio and extend it via third-party development.

Lower communications costs

Convergence in the wide area network is taking place and in the case of the backbone part of the infrastructure, IP is already the primary communications protocol. This means that CIOs can shop around in order to get the best deal. Bandwidth has become a commodity; the ability to employ one network for all media types enables economies of scale; and service providers need new revenue streams. This adds up to the ability to strike very good deals that cuts communications costs dramatically, but at the same time several service providers are operating under a financial cloud. Thus, the ability to survive in this competitive marketplace is a key issue and many organizations are already using two (or more) service providers in order to ensure continuity.

Security mechanisms

There is a perception that legacy networks are secure while those based on IP are not. This is not the case. The last mile, the physical telephony wiring that enters the organization's premises can be tapped and very expensive encryption solutions were developed in order to secure the conversations of CEOs. A plain vanilla IP network is not secure but high-level security is enabled by the IPSec standards for tunneling and encryption. Tunneling is used to establish a secure end-to-end connection, which is de facto private; encryption is employed to encode the data packets in order to retain confidentiality while they are in transit. In addition firewalls will be employed at the edge of the network and authentication techniques used to validate the identity of users and the resources they are allowed to access.

Key benefits

In addition to the reduction in communications costs, an IP VPN leverages the investment in IP platforms and applications. It is used to interconnect all sites in a secure and easy-to-manage way. Applications can be centralized at one or more sites but be employed throughout the organization. New sites can be brought on line very quickly, as can teleworkers. Private numbering schemes can be introduced, not just at the local level but throughout the organization. IP is intrinsically flexible, which eliminates the cost of adds, moves and changes. And it is future-proof: the communications protocol for video, new multimedia applications and Web-based services. IP VPNs can provide secure interconnection with third parties such as customers and key suppliers.

APPENDIX B
Returns on Investments (ROIs)

The benefits IP convergence and the migration of real time communications from circuit- to packet-switching platforms have been demonstrated in this book and entry-level migration strategies that allow those benefits to be evaluated (e.g. at a departmental level) have been covered. However, calculating the investment that will enable your organization to take optimal advantage of 21st century communications is not an easy task and in today's economic climate it is hard to overstate the importance of making the right decision. But at the same time this is not something that can be put onto the back burner. IP communications is a development that no business that wants to stay in business can afford to ignore.

The basic ROI equation is very simple. On one side there is the investment and on the other the estimated additional revenues that will be generated. From that one derives the return on investment. Additional revenues, however, come via a somewhat complex mix of lower communications and network management costs, improved productivity at the personal and workgroup levels, plus improvements in the organization's competitive edge. The keyword is estimated; for example, how much time will unified messaging really save the average employee per day? The figures in market research reports are very positive, but how relevant are they to your organization? And how can one evaluate the impact that groundbreaking applications such as communications portals and managed presence will have on the bottom line?

This may sound like a Catch 22 scenario: too good to miss but too hard to evaluate. There are any number of business models that will help with an initial assessment, but that is all they can do, and one has to be aware of the assumptions that lie behind the figures. Your own individual needs have to be discussed in detail with different vendors, that is self evident; but it is wrong to see ROI as a justification, as a kind of cut and dried decision. ROI is really a process; it does not begin and end with the acquisition of new platforms and new IP phones. In fact, one can even see ROI as a de facto product. Does it measure up to the vendor's claims? If the vendor is that confident will the company make a service level agreement? Will the figures be reevaluated when new functionality is introduced? Thus, ROI is an ongoing process.

• Returns on Investments (ROIs)

In addition, you may wish to consider investment alternatives. Vendors are beginning to offer managed services, i.e. they take full responsibility for the network and the applications. In this case there is no upfront investment and there is no need to be concerned about technical resources. This is becoming an attractive option for large enterprises that wish to focus still further on their core competence. Carriers and service providers are also moving into this area, as indicated in Appendix A. This is proving to be an attractive option for small- and medium-sized businesses, many of whom lack the requisite technical resources.

Technology is not the driver

A well-researched ROI will result in a number of technology-centric decisions. For example, the converged platform approach may be the optimum migration strategy for company 'A' while company 'B' would be better off by going directly to pure IP platforms. However, the tail should never be allowed to wag the dog: the technology should not drive the investment decision. (Note that the same technology can be applied in different ways, i.e. via customer premises equipment or a managed service.)

IP convergence does cut communications and network management costs. The total cost of ownership is lower, but applications are the primary driver. Thus, each application should be evaluated in its own right; the ROI for unified communications or managed presence, for example, has to be there regardless of the technology that enables its implementation.

Conclusions

ROIs are based on assumptions about your requirements. Check their validity.

Establish a high-level generic ROI having hard financial figures. Then drill down with an account manager, using a financial model, in order to define specific ROIs.

Once agreed, you should 'live' the agreement with the vendor. Regard ROIs as mission-critical product features; they are part of the solution's specification.

Consult on a regular basis and monitor the assumptions as well as the results.

Vendors should be willing to share the risk with a customer if an ROI is to be taken seriously.

APPENDIX C
Standards and ubiquity

IP Communications operates in an open systems environment, one that is enabled and driven by standards. Many come from the Internet, e.g. the Internet Protocol, as do developments such as the browser and instant messages. The intuitive browser interface is found on virtually all corporate desktops, but IM and the use of IP to transport voice requires modification before it can be employed by enterprises. Corporate IM systems need to be secure; quality of services mechanisms have to be introduced for VoIP. These and other issues have been or are being addressed. The solutions may be somewhat complicated and insiders may argue about the respective merits of their technology, but the momentum behind the use of one network for all media types is unstoppable.

The use of Internet standards and related technologies means that the new corporate environment is employing proven concepts that are already understood and employed by many professionals. And systems developed for the Internet address a huge market, so the optimum economies of scale are realized. Routers and LAN switches, for example, are commodity items.

Create a standard that enables the development of an innovative product that meets a real market need and everything else falls into place. The technology inside a CD player, for example, is a complex mix of computing and optical technologies that Hi-Fi magazines used to explain, but not anymore. Today it's a low-cost consumer electronics product.

The communications technology behind cellular/mobile phones is spectacular; network intelligence can locate subscribers on the other side of the globe in seconds, but today we take it for granted and that is "the true test of a technology's success; it becomes so pervasive that it disappears into the fabric of everyday life1."

Today the business case for IP Communications has to be made; the market wants proof that promises can be delivered; but tomorrow the amazing functionality that this technology enables will go down the same acceptance path.

• Standards and ubiquity

IP and related standards

TCP/IP is the protocol suite — the set of standards that underpin the Internet and all other IP-centric networks. For convenience, this acronym is often shortened to IP. As indicated earlier in the introduction, TCP/IP was designed to enable communications between disparate networks, computer hardware, operating systems and transmission media. That is why this protocol suite is mandated for use on the Internet and why it has become the lingua franca of data communications.

The fact that we accept and even expect all kinds of computers to be able to talk to each other is (or rather was) a very significant development. In the 1960s and '70s the dominant players were IBM and Digital and these two environments were radically different. IBM's architecture was vertical; dumb terminals communicating with central mainframe computers. Digital's was horizontal; computers communicated as peers over local area networks.

The situation changed when PCs started arriving on corporate desktops and we can broadly attribute the ease with which data is exchanged to the combination of Internet standards, primarily IP, and de facto standards such as Microsoft Windows. In addition, Microsoft was the driving force behind computer telephony, e.g. TAPI (Telephony API) was bundled with the operating system and the application development community immediately adopted this de facto standard. TAPI accelerated the development of call centers and the combination of TAPI and IP enabled Internet telephony, PC-to-PC, which started in the mid '90s.

Although Internet telephony was somewhat primitive at the time and call quality nowhere near good enough for real time business communications, it took the market by surprise and indicated that mainstream telephony would eventually go down the same open standards path as data communications. One can argue if the Windows environment is truly open, but published APIs do enable third-party development and that is the key benefit. And Internet standards could hardly be more open. They are set by the IETF (Internet Engineering Task Force), which was founded in 1986.

The public telephony infrastructure is obviously standards based, but circuit-switched PBXs are closed systems, which preclude the development of third-party applications, and phones are proprietary devices, i.e. they only work with the vendor's PBX. In recent years vendors started migrating towards open standards, the first move being the addition of VoIP gateways. These allow virtual private networks to replace expensive private networks. An additional benefit is the ability to extend telephony functionality out to remote sites and individual users yet at the same time manage them as if they were connected locally.

Adding converged platforms that employ both circuit- and packet-switched interfaces is a logical second move. The PBX side is proprietary; the LAN employs IP. These platforms are positioned as being best-of-both-worlds solutions that facilitate the migration to IP Communications while protecting legacy investments in PBXs, phones and cabling. These platforms will, in most cases, be based on proprietary hardware and the vendor's own real-time operating system.

Converged platforms enable telephony to become an integral part of an information and communications infrastructure, although usage is initially limited to users who connect to the IP interface and are therefore able to use their IP phones and the new IP-enhanced applications, which are hosted on the LAN. Depending on individual situations and the company's communications requirements, more and more platforms will be pure IP platforms, which run on industry-standard computer servers.

SIP (Session Initiation Protocol)

SIP may be an unfamiliar term, but this acronym is set to enter everyday parlance and take its place alongside IP and GSM. SIP is a simple, lightweight protocol that allows users to set up interactive communications sessions in a matter of seconds. It was developed in the mid-1990s by the IETF as a real time communications protocol for IP voice, and more recently it has been adopted for use in video and instant messaging applications.

Microsoft's support for SIP in Windows XP was not widely covered in the press, but the IP Communications industry recognized its significance. SIP will become a de facto call control protocol that enables communications between SIP-compliant devices. The following figure illustrates how this protocol is employed over an IP network in order to enable seamless interoperation between phones and Windows XP PCs.

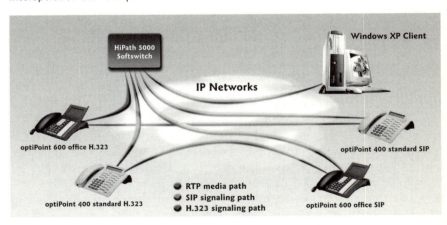

In IP Telephony SIP is used to set up communications sessions (communications links).

Unlike other call control protocols SIP puts most of the intelligence on the device, e.g. an IP phone or a PC with voice and/or IM software. This allows fully-featured, peer-to-peer communications. In traditional telephony phones are dumb devices and a central switch or server performs call processing. And because SIP is an application-layer protocol it can be accessed over any IP network. This allows seamless interoperation at the application level between wireline and wireless networks.

Ubiquitous communications and computing

So far the emphasis has been on IP Communications on wireline networks, i.e. the information and communications infrastructure of enterprises and other large organizations. However, the ability to listen to and process emails from a cellular/mobile phone indicates that: (a) the wireless side of the infrastructure is very important, particularly for mobile professionals, sales staff and maintenance technicians; and (b) the division between computing and communications is becoming increasingly blurred. Email is a data app but it can be processed using a phone using text-to-speech telephony. The phone in this case is a regular device — not an IP phone — and regular 2G circuit-switched connections are used, but the functionality from the user's perspective is that of a seamless voice-data merger and this is something that IP Communications will carry forward.

Access to information without location-centric constraints is a key requirement in today's business environment; in fact, it is rapidly becoming a competitive necessity. When information is pushed to the edge of the network it can be transferred into knowledge. Thus, the market is embracing the concept of seamless, anytime, anywhere access using any device over any network. Devices such as notebook PCs and smart phones clearly have different computing and communications resources while networks transfer data at different rates, but ubiquitous communications and computing (aka pervasive computing) are coming over the horizon.

The market opportunity is enormous. Over 40% of the average workforce is mobile and productivity would obviously be enhanced if wireline working could be replicated outside the office. On the data side this has not been possible re low transmission rates (9.6/14.4 kbps versus 10 Mbps on the LAN) and the resulting cost of 2G data calls. The situation has improved via the introduction of 2.5G services, which is packet switched; 3G is still coming over the horizon, but Wireless LAN technology has enabled a very significant advance. The original idea was to facilitate access to host resources while in the office and to enable ad hoc collaboration, e.g. exchange files when sitting round a conference table. A logical development was the deployment of the same technology in business locations such as airport lounges, conference centers, hotels and even coffee shops. These places are known as 'hot spots'.

We have the technology to realize what is no longer a vision, but we also need to change the current perception that mobility is limited to secure intranet islands within an insecure Internet cloud. There are numerous solutions that provide end-to-end security that is retained as users move between different networks and standards are emerging. But right now a key fob employing token-based authentication/encryption is highly secure as well as convenient; it can also be employed when a voice-centric device is used. This development was covered in an earlier chapter, but it is important so it is worth repeating:

The fob displays a randomly generated access code that changes every 60 seconds. The user logs on by entering a secret personal identification number (PIN) followed by the current code displayed on the display. The logon process is therefore both simple and totally secure. Nothing resides on the client device so secure access from third-party devices such as those employed in Internet cafes is enabled.

The transmission rates of hot spots are close to that of the wireline LAN and more than adequate for a mobile professional's requirements. Hot spots represent a low capex investment; they meet a market need, so they are being implemented at a staggering rate. Hot spot access is not and never will be ubiquitous, but it is an ideal complement to 2.5 and eventually 3G services. For example, a hypothetical worker pauses for a cup of coffee and downloads his/her email, including several large attachments, to a notebook PC or a PDA such as the popular iPAQ. Hot spots are therefore used when people pause, not when they are literally mobile.

When they start moving the PC/PDA loses the W-LAN signal but picks up that of a 2.5G service and new emails trickle through at the lower rate. The reverse happens when a new hot spot is encountered, which might include the mobile worker's home. This is a new development that is enabled by Mobile IP, which is basically an IP enhancement that forwards traffic to mobile users. The industry is not only working on services that enable seamless handoff and billing from one network to another, but they also retain the same secure end-to-end connection. Thus, although workers drop in and out of different networks, the service 'set' has continued to provide ubiquitous secure communications. Apart from data rates, there is no difference between working in the office, at home or out on the road; the office has been virtualized. It is no longer a physical place.

New converged devices

There is no one-size-fits-all device. Different users have different needs and those needs vary. A mobile phone may suffice when away from the office for an hour or so; at other times the same person may carry a phone and a PDA; notebook PCs will normally be carried on business trips together with the phone. Thus, there are various wireless horses for various wireless courses. In addition, the key fob described in the previous chapter enables secure access from third party devices, e.g. business centers in hotels, Internet cafes, Internet PCs at conferences and exhibitions. In these cases mobile users get high-speed access at a significant cost saving — free at times.

• Standards and ubiquity

One can distinguish between people who are voice centric and those that are data centric. The former category is well served by unified communications solutions and communications portals. There are a number of 'smart' phones that have data capabilities but the small screen is an obvious limitation, as are the limited computing resources. Smart phones using the WAP interface were hyped to the hilt a few years ago, but these devices turned into an expensive, marketing flop.

The second category is well served by PDAs such as the iPAQ and similar devices running Windows Pocket PC. Functionality can be expanded via plug-in modules, which allows users to pack whatever they need at the time. For example, the hot-spot access module would typically not be carried for short trips. Modules are also used to expand the memory and a small keyboard can be employed for PC-type tasks. These versatile devices can therefore function as a notebook PC and in addition wireless telephone calls can be made.

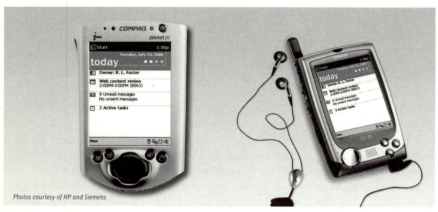

Photos courtesy of HP and Siemens

The popular iPAQ PDA (left) has computing resources that match those of earlier desktop PCs. Memory, for example, can be expanded to 1GB. PDAs can also be used for telephony, as shown (right) on another Windows Pocket PDA.

Telephony would normally be done using an earpiece, which many business professionals employ. In future small wireless headsets that employ short-range Bluetooth technology will probably be used. These remove the need for a wireline link and many PDAs already have Bluetooth interfaces since this is a convenient way of synchronizing information with desktop/notebook PCs.

This wireless set-up is known as a PAN (Personal Area Network) and it is a concept that really does match the mobility paradigm. To make a call you simply tap on the relevant entry in the address book; incoming calls are immediately identified if that person is in the book.

Other devices having similar functionality include: the BlackBerry, Pocket PC phone edition, T-Mobile's Sidekick and Danger.

Intelligent network services

Unified communications and communications portals are intelligent network services. The model is still client-server, but communications are interactive. For example, instead of downloading emails to the client, processing them and sending the replies back to the server the emails stay on the server and are processed via commands. When a phone is used the mobile user can listen to his/her email and give interactive commands such as next, delete and reply. This is enabled by text-to-speech technology. When a PDA is used the contents of the email are displayed and they are processed via a small keyboard that sends interactive data commands back to the server.

Thus, the communications link stays open for the duration of the session and traffic goes back and forth. This would be an expensive way of working in a circuit-switched network; the communications link would be dedicated to the needs of a single user and it would be charged on a time and distance model. In packet-switched network communications resources are shared and the charge will typically be based on the amount of data transmitted. As well as being cheaper, packet-switched IP Communications means that the client device no longer needs to have powerful computing resources.

Photo courtesy of Research in Motion.

The popularity of the BlackBerry PDA has led to the development of intelligent wireless email services that display senders and subjects as well as the contents of attachments. Emails are not downloaded; instead the user works directly with the server. This kind of online communications is particularly useful and cost-effective over a wireless IP network, e.g. 2.5G. The BlackBerry can also be used for telephony, so it is an ideal multi-modal device.

Related developments allow thin-client devices to display the contents of attachments. If an email has a large Word attachment, for example, or if a fax has been received, the user can scroll through the file, reading it line by line; there is no need to make a lengthy download.

• Standards and ubiquity

The combination of these new converged devices and intelligent network services is the closest thing yet to a perfect mobility match. You 'wear' a personal area network, employ a graphical interface for telephony, can use voice or data commands to do email, maybe add a keyboard to do some serious writing, and don't get hit with a big phone bill at the end of the month.

GLOSSARY
Glossary of terms used in this book

2G/2.5G and 3G. These are cellular telephony terms that are associated with the GSM digital set of standards. IG (the first generation) refers to analog standards; 2G is digital (the basis of today's wireless networks); 2.5G adds packet-switched data; 3G promises higher data transfer rates.

API: Application Programming Interface. These are rules that allow application software to communicate with the operating system. APIs eliminate the need to for programmers to be concerned with hardware and networks.

ATM: Asynchronous Transfer Mode. This is a telecommunications packet switching technology; the packets are known as cells. There are similarities to IP but a key difference is the fact that ATM establishes a temporary permanent circuit through the network.

Bluetooth: Bluetooth is the name given to a short-range (100 meters) wireless interface standard designed primarily to enable the transfer of voice and data between mobile devices (laptops, PDAs, phones) and desktop machines. The name Bluetooth comes from King Harald Blatan (Bluetooth) of Denmark, who lived in the 10th century.

CRM: Customer Relationship Management. Systems used to plan, schedule and control pre- and post-sales activities. Call centers are normally linked to back-office CRM systems.

CTI: Computer Telephony Integration. CTI refers to the technology and applications that link traditional voice and data environments. Call centers are CTI systems.

DOS: Disk Operating System. Microsoft Windows replaced DOS on PCs.

ERP: Enterprise Resource Planning. Originally a manufacturing system but one that now comprises virtually all related activities.

Hot spot: Used to denote availability of Wi-Fi access to the Internet in a public place.

IETF: Internet Engineering Task Force. This is the group that sets Internet standards.

• Glossary

IP: Internet Protocol. IP is the lingua franca of data communications; it is part of the TCP/IP set of communications protocols. This protocol is widely used on local and wide area networks.

IP PBXs provide similar functionality to legacy PBXs but employ a different switching technology.

IPSec. Standards used to provide tunneling and encryption over an IP network. Employed in VPNs.

IM: Instant Messages. This is a relatively new communications medium, particularly for the corporate environment. Its origins are that of the Internet.

ISDN: Integrated Services Digital Network. The two services were digital voice and data. This is a well-established standard but the basic transmission rate of 64 kbps is too low for today's market.

LAN: Local Area Network. LANs provide data connectivity inside a designated area, typically and office. Computer servers and client devices (PCs) connect to LANs.

Latency: this is the average time it takes for a packet to travel from the source to the destination.

Linux: this is an open source (free) version of UNIX. IBM and other computer companies support this OS standard.

OS: Operating System. DOS, Microsoft Windows and UNIX are operating systems.

PBX: Private Branch Exchange. An in-house telephony system that connects, disconnects, and transfers calls.

PDA: Personal Digital Assistant, e.g. the Palm Pilot or HP-Compaq iPAQ.

PSTN: Public Switched Telephony Network; the global infrastructure that handles telephone calls.

QoS (Quality of Service) is the key VoIP issue. This is a broad term used to describe mechanisms that (a) detect that the data packets are those of a real-time medium (voice or video) and (b) that route the packets according to their priority.

Softphone: PC or PDA that runs IP telephony software. Can be used as a phone or in combination with an IP phone, e.g. computing resources and graphical interfaces are used to facilitate advanced telephony applications such as conferencing

SIP: (Session Initiation Protocol). This lightweight, flexible protocol is used to set up communication sessions (communication links) and it is widely employed in converged voice-data applications. SIP is bundled in the Windows XP operating system.

SMS: Short Message Service. Originally designed to inform mobile phone users that they had voicemail. Became popular with young subscribers having pre-paid accounts.

TAPI: Telephony API developed by Microsoft and Intel in 1993. It shipped with Windows 95. TAPI is basically a front-end interface for telephony applications.

TSAPI: Telephony Services API. An API was developed by Novel and AT&T; it predates TAPI.

TCP/IP: The packets that TCP/IP routes contain the destination address and the destination network. Thus, messages can be sent to multiple networks. This is known as multicasting, i.e. information is sent to specific groups.

UC Unified Communications The addition of real-time communications (telephony) functionality to unified messaging, e.g. the ability to listen to emails from a cellular phone

UM Unified Messaging An inbox such as Microsoft Exchange or Lotus Notes that contains all messaging media types: email, facsimile and voicemail. May also include SMS

UNIX: a multi-user, multi-tasking operating system originally used on mini computers. UNIX was developed at the bell (AT&T) laboratories in 1969.

USB: Universal Serial Bus. A PC interface used for low-speed peripherals.

VoIP: Voice over IP. This indicates that the voice signal has been digitized and converted into the packet format used by IP. The digital bandwidth for voice over IP can be less than 1/16th that of the PSTN.

VPN: Virtual Private Network. A way of employing a public network so that it appears to be private. Tunneling, as enabled by IPSec, provides this function.

WAN Wide Area Network. A corporate WAN is formed by LANs that are interconnected with a VPN.

W-LAN Wireless LAN. The term Wi-Fi is also employed to describe W-LAN systems although the correct use is to indicate that the system meets the standard and will interoperate with the systems of other Wi-Fi compliant vendors